KU-209-754

Observer FINAL EDITION

QUIT!

Doenitz Orders All Fighting Forces to Surrender to Allies

FRIday FIELD·DAY

The Daily Telegraph
and Morning Post

CHURCHILL RESIGNS: ATTLEE PREMIER

SOCIALISTS GET CLEAR MAJORITY OF 153

LEADER LIKELY TO GO TO POTSDAM TO-DAY

NAMES OF NEW CABINET TO BE ISSUED AT ONCE

JAPAN GIVEN CHANCE TO SURRENDER

PROCLAMATION BY BRITAIN, U.S. AND CHINA

GOOD WHISKY Johnnie Walker

DAILY EXPRESS One Penny
SATURDAY MAY 12 1945

DEMOB. DAY—JUNE 18

in Forces to be freed

Jap peace feelers

THIS IS HOW MOSCOW WELCOMED THE BRITISH ON VE DAY

COVENTRY WAS MY WORK

Churchill may hint at election date

MEAT RATION WILL BE CUT

News Chronicle LATE LONDON EDITION One Penny
FRIDAY, JULY 27, 1945

WAS ABSOLUTE MAJORITY OF 167

BECOMES PREMIER, WILL

POTSDAM

World is taken aback by the new

THE ELECTION IN BRIEF

Government—208 seats

	Gains	Losses	Net	New House	Old House
CONSERVATIVES	7	183	—176	194	358
NATIONAL	—	5	—5	1	9
SIMONITES	1	15	—14	13	27
TOTALS	8	203	—195	208	394

Opposition—411 seats

LABOUR	214	3	—211	393	163
LIBERALS	4	11	—7	10	19
*OTHERS	1	5	—4	8	10
TOTALS	219	19	—200	411	192

*Include I.L.P., Communist, Common Wealth

Independents—8 seats

Includes two Irish Nationalists

	6	—	6	8	22

Seats to be declared 13 · 627 · 640 · 615

Full results of the election on Pages Three, Four and Five

Evening Standard FINAL
BIRD'S CUSTARD

Britain swings to the Left—and the Churchill Government goes out in a landslide

SOCIALISTS IN

26 Ministers go down

LONDON, BIRMINGHAM CAPTURED: LIBERALS ECLIPSED

STATE OF PARTIES

MINISTERS DEFEATED

MR. EDEN'S BIG MAJORITY

BEVIN AND MORRISON IN

NEW PRIME MINISTER

The next step

The Socialists win London

The Wiltshire anthem

Left to fight his campaign

Election results in full are on Pages Three, Four, Five and Eight

VE DAY

VICTORY IN EUROPE 1945

May 19, 1945

PICTURE POST

THE START OF VE-DAY

HULTON'S NATIONAL WEEKLY

In this issue :

VICTORY SPECIAL 4ᴰ

MAY 19, 1945

Vol. 27. No. 7

VE DAY

VICTORY IN EUROPE 1945

ROBIN CROSS

Guild Publishing, London
in association with
The Imperial War Museum
London

This edition published 1985 by
Book Club Associates
by arrangement with Sidgwick & Jackson Ltd

© Copyright Sidgwick & Jackson Ltd 1985

Produced by Charles Herridge Ltd

Picture research by Jenny de Gex

Typeset by P&M Typesetting Ltd, Exeter,
Devon

Colour reproduction by Anglia Reproductions,
Witham, Essex

Printed in Italy by New Interlitho SpA, Milan

The author would particularly like to thank the
staff of the Mass-Observation Archive, the staff
of the reference library of the Imperial War
Museum and Jenny de Gex for their invaluable
help in the preparation of this book.

CONTENTS

Part One

A WORLD IN FLAMES

'We shall never capitulate, no never. We may be destroyed, but if we are, we shall drag a world with us, a world in flames.' Adolf Hitler, 1943

IN THE WOLF'S LAIR

From the beginning of the Russian campaign, which had opened on 22 June 1941, Adolf Hitler had steadily withdrawn into a world of his own creation. On the evening of 23 November 1942 – as General Friedrich von Paulus' German 6th Army found itself trapped in a giant Soviet encirclement west of Stalingrad – the Fuehrer returned to his headquarters (FHQ, *Fuehrerhauptquartier*) at Rastenburg in East Prussia, set deep in the gloomy, dripping pine forests of the Masurian lakes. With the exception of a brief period in February-March 1943 spent at the FHQ at Vinnitsa in the Ukraine, and occasional trips to Berlin, Berchtesgaden and Munich, Hitler was to remain in residence at Rastenburg until November 1944.

The FHQ at Rastenburg was codenamed *Wolfsschanze*, 'The Wolf's Lair'. Few headquarters have reflected so accurately the psychology of a supreme commander. After the war General Jodl, the chief of Hitler's personal staff, recalled Rastenburg as a 'cross between a cloister and a concentration camp'. Built in 1941, the Wolf's Lair was protected by belts of mines and barbed wire. The FHQ itself – situated in Security Zone One – was a massive concrete block-house, aptly described as resembling a 'primitive sarcophagus'. No sunlight penetrated its 22ft thick walls, and the only direct ventilation came when its vast iron doors slowly swung open. Inside, its small, plainly furnished rooms were far removed from the grandiose vistas of Nuremberg and the stilted pomp of the Berlin Reich Chancellery. The overall impression at Rastenburg was one of monotony and melancholy. After a visit the Italian Foreign Minister, Count Ciano, wrote, 'One does not see a single colourful spot, nor a single lively touch. The ante-rooms are full of people smoking, eating and chatting. Smell of kitchens, uniforms, heavy boots.'

The climate was atrocious – freezing in winter, oppressively hot and mosquito-ridden in summer, the nights throbbing with the croaking of bullfrogs. In an effort to control the mosquitoes, kerosene was poured on all the surrounding lakes, but this also killed off all the frogs, in the process enraging Hitler, who claimed that their deafening serenade lulled him to sleep at night. An expedition was mounted to restock the area with bullfrogs from more distant lakes.

It was in these bleak surroundings that Hitler settled into the abstract world of military maps and situation conferences. As the initiative passed from Germany into the hands of the Red Army and the Western Allies, his contact with military reality shrank to the contours and configurations of the maps on his conference table. Everything else was excluded from the hermetically sealed atmosphere of Security Zone One. As Jodl recalled, 'Apart from reports on the military situation, very little news from the outside world penetrated the FHQ.' Hitler began each day by poring over specially prepared press excerpts. Distressing items were removed.

The ruins of Caen, photographed in 1945.

After Stalingrad the Fuehrer's nerves became increasingly shredded and his health declined. As the months went by, each day became a grinding exercise in self-control. As early as May 1942, Josef Goebbels had been shocked by Hitler's physical appearance: 'I noted that he had become quite grey and that merely talking about the cares of winter makes him seem to have aged very much.' In 1943, Hitler began to suffer from a convulsive trembling of his left arm and leg. The sunlight bothered him, and on his short walks in the Rastenburg compound he wore a cap with a specially enlarged visor. Frequently he complained about the gradual loss of his sense of balance – 'I always have the feeling of tipping away to the right'.

Hitler at the map table in the Wolf's Lair.

Morbidly guzzling the patent pills provided by his personal physician, the quack Morell, and sustained by the endless round of conferences, Hitler now embarked on a long, regressive interior journey. As Goebbels wrote, 'He no longer gets out in the fresh air, no longer has any relaxation; he sits in his bunker, acts and broods....' The layers of success were peeled away one by one to reveal intact the visionary and dreamer of the 1920s. Since the failure of the 1923 Munich putsch Hitler had repeatedly recharged his energies and maintained his impetus by seeking out and confronting fresh crises. Now the war was to be one prolonged crisis, a gigantic projection of the struggles in his rise to power. There were to be brief remissions but the condition of the patient was already terminal.

LOST VICTORIES

In the middle of June 1944 it was clear that Germany was facing defeat. In the east the great buffer of territory acquired in the victorious campaigns of 1941 and 1942 had been remorselessly eaten away by the bludgeoning series of Soviet offensives which began at Kursk in July 1943 and, ten months later, slithered to a halt in the April mud of 1944. On 5 January the Russians had crossed their pre-war

Mud, horses and armour, three of the constant factors on the Eastern Front. Plodding alongside a PzKpfw VI Tiger heavy battle tank are two of the two and a half million horses used by the Germans in the east during the course of the war. About 80 per cent of the Wehrmacht depended on the horse for its motive power and losses were about 1,000 a day.

frontier with Poland at Rokitno, marking the beginning of their advance into western Europe. Four months later they had recovered virtually all of their pre-war territory lost in the campaigns of 1941-42. Now the Red Army was a bare 50 miles from that part of the River Bug which the Wehrmacht had crossed on the second day of Barbarossa, 23 June 1941. In the autumn of 1943 the Stavka (Russian high command) estimated that the Wehrmacht deployed more than 60 per cent of its total strength – and more than 50 per cent of all its armour – on the Eastern Front, 236 divisions in all. In the crucial battle for the western Ukraine, Stalin had defeated the Wehrmacht on the very ground over which the Red Army had been so comprehensively outmanoeuvred and outfought in 1941 and 1942. In the winter campaigns of 1943-44 the Russians inflicted a million casualties on the German armies and those of their allies. Only one army had been lost at Stalingrad, but in this period four armies – 6th, 8th, 16th and 18th – were wrecked beyond recall and the 17th Army left to its fate trapped in the Crimea. After the terrible battering of the winter only Army Group Centre could field a fully operational Panzer army. But even here General Busch was left to contemplate a 650-mile front on which there was only one division of about 2,000 men to every 16 miles. The Eastern Front was now increasingly shored up with 60 divisions of 'satellite' armies – Hungarian, German/Russian and Rumanian, many of them as hostile towards each other as they were fearful of the Russians.

The autumn and winter campaigns of 1943-44 had stretched the Red Army to the limit. After the war Major-General von Mellenthin, a veteran of the Eastern Front, wrote of the fighting in the Kiev salient: 'There is no doubt that at this stage of the war the Russians collared for the ordinary infantry divisions anyone, regardless of training, health or age – and sometimes of sex – and pushed them ruthlessly into battle ... in this grim month of December 1943 the German soldiers

The Tiger in action during the fighting in the Kursk salient, July 1943. In the last great German offensive of the war Hitler's finest panzer divisions were bled white in the Red Army's deeply echeloned defensive positions. Among the armoured divisions most grievously mangled in the Kursk salient was 3rd Panzer, which found itself left with 30 tanks out of 300. Overall German tank losses were in the region of 2,500.

A PzKpfw V Panther main battle tank of Panzer Corps *Grossdeutschland* churns through the high summer dust on the Eastern Front, August 1944. The Panther first saw action at Kursk, where it proved to be very unreliable. Many tanks broke down before they reached the front. Once problems with the engine, transmission and suspension were overcome, the Panther became the equal of the Red Army's T-34.

A German soldier examines a captured Soviet T-34 in the summer of 1942. The Russian tank arm's disastrous baptism of fire forced a major reorganization, beginning with the formation of five 'tank armies' at the beginning of 1943.

in the Ukraine felt a flicker of hope ... the Russians could not continue to suffer these huge losses indefinitely.' Hope flickered eternal in the German lines, but the Russian war machine ground relentlessly on. Von Manstein estimated that, between July 1943 and January 1944, the Soviets in the south had received just over a million men and 2,700 tanks (including assault guns) to replace 405,409 killed, wounded or missing and an unknown loss of armoured vehicles. All Hitler could offer was empty promises and a Christmas present of 50 tanks to General von Manteuffel, one of his favourite commanders.

The single most significant casualty of the winter campaign was the commander of Army Group South, Field Marshal von Manstein, the ablest of all Hitler's generals. Under extreme pressure, Manstein had displayed superb generalship in conducting a step by step retreat to the Polish frontier. He was never afraid to tell Hitler that he was wrong, and the vigour with which he supported his arguments eventually became too much for the Fuehrer and Himmler, who considered him politically unsound. Manstein stood up to Hitler for the last time on 25 March 1944, over the extrication of 1st Panzer Army from a Soviet encirclement south-east of Tarnopol. Manstein won the argument but within a week he had been removed from his command and replaced by Field Marshal Model. Manstein's departure coincided with the redesignation of Army Groups South and A as, respectively, Army Groups North and Southern Ukraine. The new names had a hollow ring for little of the Ukraine now remained in German hands.

A WAR ON TWO FRONTS

In June 1944 Army Group Centre still held the Vitebsk 'Gate', the gap between the headwaters of the Dvina and Dniepr rivers. From Vitebsk to Berlin was a distance of 750 miles, only 100 miles further than the distance from Normandy's Cotentin Peninsula to the capital of the Third Reich. In Normandy the Germans had failed successively to prevent, defeat and contain the Allied invasion of France. On 12 June the Allied bridgehead became continuous when 101st American Airborne Division captured Carentan, which commands the estuary of the Vire. This closed the last gap in the Allied front, between Omaha and Utah beaches, linking their forces together in a beachhead 42 miles wide.

Once the Allies had established their bridgehead the outcome was not only inevitable but hastened by Hitler's refusal to listen to the advice of his commanders or to release divisions of 15th Army – stationed north of the Seine – because of his belief that the Allies would make a second landing in the Pas de Calais. As Field Marshal von Rundstedt, Commander-in-Chief West at the time of the invasion, reflected after the war: 'I knew all along that the German position in France was hopeless and that eventually the war would be lost. But if I had been given a free hand to conduct operations, I think I could have made the Allies pay a fearful price for their victory. I had planned to fight a slow retiring action, exacting a heavy toll for each bit of ground I gave up. I had hoped that this might have brought about a political decision which would have saved Germany from complete and utter defeat. But I did not have my way. As commander-in-chief in the west my only authority was to change the guard in front of my gate.'

US infantry in action in the lanes of the 'bocage' country near St Lô, 18 July 1944.

Vehicles of a US infantry division move through the wreckage of St Lô, which was secured after heavy fighting on 18 July 1944.

On 17 June Hitler travelled to Margival, near Soissons, for a conference with von Rundstedt and Field Marshal Rommel, commander of Army Group B. The conference was held in the elaborate underground command headquarters prepared in the summer of 1940 for the invasion of Britain. Now the sea wall of 'Fortress Europe' had been breached and the tide was flowing irresistibly back to Germany. General Speidel, Rommel's chief of staff, noted that Hitler 'looked pale and sleepless. He played nervously with his glasses and with pencils of all colours, which he held in his hand. He was the only one seated, hunched on a stool, while the field marshals were kept standing. His earlier magnetic force seemed gone.'

Rommel explained the deepening crisis – the overwhelming superiority of the enemy air force, the near impossibility of making daylight troop movements and the continuing build-up in the bridgehead. He urged Hitler to release the 15 to 20 divisions stationed in southern France and on the Atlantic coast to reinforce a counter-offensive in Normandy. The Fuehrer swept the plea aside. For Hitler there was only one strategy – 'no withdrawal'. Not a foot of ground must be surrendered voluntarily. Clinging to the belief that the Allies could still be flung back into the sea, he embarked on a long Fuehrer lecture, promising his commanders masses of 'turbo' fighters which would sweep the Allied aircraft from the sky, and drooling over the imminent prospect of a London laid waste by his V-1 flying bombs. That night he left for Berchtesgaden after one of his new 'revenge weapons' had blown up on a nearby launching pad. Three days later von Rundstedt received a detailed new Fuehrer plan for a grand offensive by four Waffen SS and two army panzer divisions 'to destroy the American forces at Balleroy – after the British had been annihilated at Orne'.

Hitler's absolute determination to deny the Allies access to the open country beyond the bridgehead, wearing them down by a process of attrition, only ensured the piecemeal destruction of his best armoured forces at the forward point of contact with the enemy. In the slugging match which developed around Caen, it was not the British who were annihilated, but the massive concentration of SS armour at Cheux, 12 miles west of Caen, which on 29 June was savagely mauled by an intense air and artillery bombardment as it launched a counter-attack on the right flank of the British 8th Corps. German strategy had rested on the hope that an armoured force could be assembled in sufficient strength to crush the Allies. On 29 June it had itself been crushed even before it had gained any momentum. Now there was no more armour to feed into the battle.

After the debacle in the Cheux salient von Rundstedt recognized that the war was lost. When Jodl asked him, 'What shall we do?' he replied, 'End the war. What else can we do?' This frankness resulted in his dismissal on 2 July and replacement by Field Marshal von Kluge, a tough veteran of the Eastern Front who arrived in Normandy full of optimisim but was soon disillusioned. On 18 June US 7th Corps had reached the suburbs of Cherbourg. A bitter fight for the city and its port lasted until the 27th when organized resistance finally collapsed. Two days later the last German-held strongpoint on Cherbourg's breakwater surrendered. With Cherbourg secured, the Allies prepared to turn eastward against a German left flank

The men who planned and directed Overlord, the Allied invasion of north-west Europe, photographed in February 1944. From left to right: Lieutenant-General Omar Bradley, Admiral Sir Bertram Ramsay, Air Chief Marshal Sir Arthur Tedder, General Dwight D. Eisenhower, General Sir Bernard Montgomery, Air Chief Marshal Sir Trafford Leigh Mallory and Lieutenant-General Walter Bedell Smith.

General Sir Alan Brooke, Churchill and Montgomery at the latter's HQ in Normandy.

weakened by the concentration of seven of their ten panzer divisions in the fighting at Caen. Caen finally fell on 9 July. Nine days later British and Canadian troops broke through south-east of the shattered town, picking their way through the rubble and destruction left in the wake of an aerial bombardment delivered by 2,200 aircraft which dropped over 7,000 tons of bombs.

THE BOMB PLOT

On 24 July von Kluge reported that the German losses in the previous five weeks of fighting were more than 2,000 tanks, 340 aircraft and 113,000 men. Reinforcements amounted to only 10,000 men. Meanwhile the enemy's losses were 'immediately replaced'. One irreplaceable loss had been Field Marshal Rommel, who had been badly injured on 17 July when his car was shot up by an enemy fighter. Rommel had no illusions about the situation in Normandy. In a letter to Hitler of 21 July, von Kluge included observations by Rommel which concluded with this warning: 'The force is fighting heroically everywhere, but the unequal combat is nearing its end. It is in my opinion necessary to draw the appropriate conclusions from the situation.' To General Speidel Rommel had remarked, 'If he [Hitler] draws no conclusions we shall act.' Rommel had established contact with the group of conspirators around General Beck and Carl Goerdeler, the former mayor of Leipzig. They planned to seize Hitler and try him before a German court. Rommel would assume command of the armed forces and negotiate with Eisenhower while continuing to fight in the east.

Stauffenberg (far left) with Hitler at the Wolf's Lair a few days before the attempted assassination. Keitel is on the right.

While Rommel lay unconscious in a military hospital, action was taken, not to arrest Hitler but to kill him. Several unsuccessful attempts on the Fuehrer's life had already been made by his military opposition. The nearest they had come to killing him was on 13 March, when a time bomb placed in Hitler's plane by General Henning von Tresckow and Lieutenant Fabian von Schlabrendorff failed to explode. On 20 July Colonel Claus Schenk von Stauffenberg, chief of staff to the Reserve Army, arrived at Rastenburg to attend a military briefing. In his briefcase he carried a bomb. Stauffenberg had already been forced to abandon assassination plans on three separate occasions. Now there was an added urgency to his mission, for on 17 July had come news of the imminent arrest of Carl Goerdeler.

Stauffenberg primed the bomb before going into the conference, which was being held in a wooden barrack hut next to Hitler's concrete bunker. He slid the briefcase under the heavy wooden table over which Hitler was leaning, intently studying maps. Then, excusing himself to make a telephone call, he left. A few minutes later, at 12.42pm, he watched from his readied car as a loud explosion tore the hut apart, sending shards of wood and sheets of paper whirling skywards in a black column of smoke. In the confusion which followed the explosion he bluffed his way out of the Wolf's Lair and flew back to Berlin, convinced that Hitler was dead.

Had Stauffenberg waited, he would have seen Hitler – his face blackened, hair scorched and uniform in tatters – stagger from the wrecked building on the arm of Field Marshal Keitel. He had been saved by the heavy wooden table top and the thin walls of the barrack hut, which had failed to confine the blast. Four of those attending the conference died of their wounds but Hitler suffered only minor injuries, a bruised back and hands, burst eardrums and splinters in his legs. In the sudden euphoria of his escape he found that the trembling in his left leg had largely ceased. Later that day he was able to receive Mussolini at the headquarters railway station, excitedly telling him, 'After my miraculous escape from death today I am more than ever convinced that it is my fate to bring our common enterprise to a successful conclusion.'

In Berlin, where Stauffenberg's fellow conspirators waited in the War Ministry, there was a fatal delay. Communications with Rastenburg were eventually restored and it became clear that Hitler was still alive. It was not until late in the afternoon – following the gallant Stauffenberg's arrival – that any attempt was made to launch their *putsch* and place the most dangerous elements of the Nazi

Hitler shows Mussolini the wrecked conference room.

apparatus, the SS, under arrest. But by now the momentary opportunity for 'Operation Valkyrie' had passed.

Isolated, irresolute and lacking the support of large numbers of troops to put their orders into effect, the conspirators had let their chance slip. They came close to success only in Paris, where General von Stülpnagel succeeded in rounding up the SS and Gestapo. But his commander, von Kluge, would not support him and when news arrived that Hitler was alive, they were released. In the unreal atmosphere which prevailed they drank champagne with their former captors.

As darkness fell in Berlin there was a confused series of shootings. The plotters attempted to eliminate officials loyal to Hitler. Then, as the tide turned, those who remained loyal – or who, like Stauffenberg's superior General Fromm, were still sitting on the fence – tried as rapidly as possible to demonstrate their allegiance to the Fuehrer and to dispose of any survivors of Valkyrie who might implicate them in the affair. Fromm ordered the execution of Stauffenberg and three other officers, and they were shot in the courtyard of the War Ministry by the light of an armoured car's headlamps. He was only prevented from eliminating more of the plotters on the spot by the arrival of Himmler's lieutenant Kaltenbrunner, who was more interested in interrogation than execution.

Shortly before lam Hitler's shaky but instantly recognizable voice spoke on the radio to the German people. He left his listeners in no doubt as to the fate of the conspirators: 'This time we shall get even with them in the way to which we National Socialists are accustomed.' Revenge was swift and terrible. The wave of arrests and executions which followed swept up two field marshals and 16 generals. Some attempted suicide. On his way back to face trial and certain death in Germany General von Stülpnagel requested to go by way of Verdun, where he had commanded a battalion in 1916. He stopped to look at the battlefield, stepped from his car and walked out of sight. The driver heard a shot and found von Stülpnagel floating face down in a canal. He had tried to kill himself but had only succeeded in putting out his eyes, a grim postscript to the plotters' ineffectuality. Blind and helpless, he went to his death in Berlin. Henning von Tresckow killed himself, but his corpse was dragged from the family vault and taken to Berlin, where it was displayed at interrogations to break his former colleagues' morale. Fromm's belated display of loyalty failed to save him. He was arrested by the Gestapo, tortured, and executed in March 1945.

The first executions took place in the Plötzensee prison on 8 August. Field Marshal von Witzleben and Generals Höpner, Hase and Stieff, together with four other officers, were put to death with the utmost barbarity, by slow hanging from a meathook. The proceedings were filmed and watched that night by Hitler.

Probably about 5,000 were executed after the bomb plot, and right up to the end of the war a '20 July Special Commission' was rooting out suspects. Many of the conspirators' families – including those of Stauffenberg and Goerdeler – were arrested en masse. It was to save his family from this fate that, in October, Rommel took the poison offered him by the Fuehrer's emissary General Burgdorf rather than face a military 'court of honour' and then trial in the People's Court. Rommel was buried with full military honours. In the funeral oration von Rundstedt said, 'His heart belongs to the Fuehrer'.

In the aftermath of the bomb plot came the humiliation of what

General von Witzleben at his trial before the People's Court following the bomb plot. Witzleben presented a harrowing sight. Completely shattered and deprived of his braces, he was forced to hold up his trousers when ordered to stand. He was executed in barbaric circumstances on 8 August 1944.

remained of the Army General Staff and its command organization. Henceforth it was completely subordinated to the SS, who assumed control of the raising, equipping and training of army formations. Heinrich Himmler was appointed commander-in-chief of the Reserve Army. It was Hitler's final victory over the hated aristocrats of the General Staff.

HITLER'S SECRET WEAPONS

In Hitler the assassination attempt seemed to release a previously untapped source of energy. The new chief of the General Staff, Guderian, reflected, 'All the forces that lurked within him were aroused and came into their own. He recognized no limits any more.' But at the same time Hitler slid into the apocalyptic fantasy world in which 'anyone who speaks to me of peace without victory will lose his head'. Hitler now placed his hopes for victory in the secret weapons he had promised his generals at Soissons. The first V-1 flying bombs had chugged across the Channel in the small hours of 13 June. They came as a complete surprise to the British public, who at first assumed that they were downed enemy aircraft. Ten days later the Home Secretary Herbert Morrison announced that pilotless aircraft were being used against the British Isles and went on to warn, 'When the engine... stops and the light at the end of the machine is seen to go out, it may mean that an explosion will soon follow, perhaps in five to fifteen seconds.'

As the V-1 bombardment continued, Londoners cultivated a determinedly casual attitude to this new threat. One woman recalled, 'having lunch one day in a small restaurant in Baker St when the ominous sound of a doodle-bug was heard and it got nearer and louder. Everyone in the restaurant gradually stopped talking and eating and froze, with knives and forks poised in mid-air until we all looked like statues. Then the usual bang was heard as a doodle-bug landed somewhere nearby, and it was wonderful to see everyone just carrying on eating and taking up their conversations without even referring to what had happened.'

To combat the V-1s, London's anti-aircraft defences were moved to the south-coast, and squadrons of fighters patrolled what became known as 'flying bomb alley' above the fields of Sussex and Kent. As a

A V-1 about to plunge into central London, 28 June 1944.

long stop an immense balloon barrage was set up on the approach to London along the 20-mile ridge between Cobham and Limpsfield. Directly beneath the barrage lay the village of Eynsford, which was the regular Sunday afternoon destination of a woman from the south London suburbs. 'There was a splendid view ... We could see the little hamlets nestling in the valleys ... we could hear the larks singing ... and we could look up and see the massive balloon barrage. If the sirens sounded, we could watch with a feeling of detachment as the "buzz bombs" roared over, seeming to thread their way between the balloons. Later on we would cycle home, often to find the house blown inside out again and fresh holes in the roof.'

Of the 9,000 V-1 firings between June and September 1944, a quarter failed to cross the coast and only a quarter got near the capital. Croydon seemed to be their favourite flight path – one vigilant dentist counted 37 passing over his surgery during the course of a single day. Just under 6,200 people were killed by the doodle-bugs and 18,000 seriously injured. In September, as their launching sites were overrun, they gave way to the V-2 rocket.

THE ALLIES PUSH ON

The V-1 campaign was unnerving for Londoners, but had no effect on the progress of the fighting in France. On 31 July Avranches fell to the US 8th Corps. Von Kluge informed Hitler: 'Whether the enemy can still be stopped at this point is questionable. The enemy air superiority is terrific, and smothers almost every one of our movements ... Losses in men and equipment are extraordinary. The morale of the troops has suffered very heavily under constant murderous enemy fire, especially since all infantry units consist only of haphazard groups which do not form a strongly co-ordinated force any longer. In the rear areas of the front, terrorists, feeling the end approaching, grow steadily bolder.'

In the next two weeks the American breakout surged ahead as General Patton's US 3rd Army fanned out virtually unopposed along the roads from Avranches west to Brest, south to Nantes and east to Le Mans and beyond. Hitler refused to allow von Kluge to fall back on the

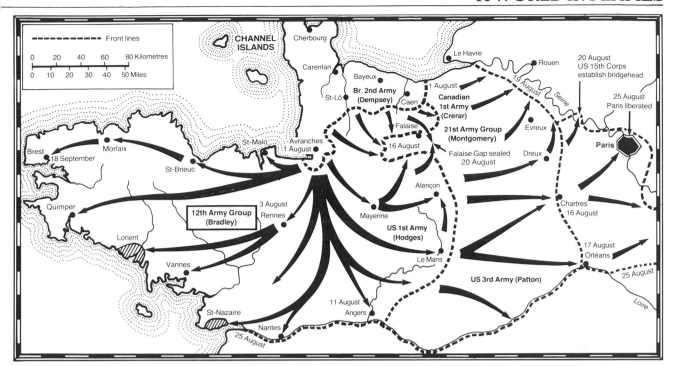

The Normandy break-out.

below Some of the 50,000 German troops taken prisoner in the battle of the Falaise Gap, which came to an end on 20 August 1944. On the next day men of Patton's US 3rd Army crossed the Seine.

Seine but instead ordered him to throw in an armoured attack on the American lines of communication at Avranches. The Fuehrer supplied him with a detailed plan but no reinforcements. The attack went in but within three days had been stopped at Mortain and rolled back to its start line. The failure of the attack at Mortain trapped 100,000 men of 5th Panzer Army, 7th Army and Panzer Group Eberbach in a salient between Falaise and Argentan which was being sealed off in the north by Crerar's Canadian 1st Army and in the south by

Patton's US 3rd Army. By the evening of 17 August the jaws of the pincer were only six miles apart. Three days later they finally snapped shut on 50,000 German troops, thousands of trucks and over 5,000 armoured vehicles.

Another casualty of the battle for the Falaise gap was Field Marshal von Kluge. On 15 August, while he was in the front line near Avranches, his wireless tender was knocked out, cutting off communications with his headquarters for several hours. At Rastenburg, where von Kluge was already a marked man, it was assumed that he was trying to negotiate with the Allies. On the 17th he was relieved of his command and received the dreaded order to return to Germany. On the way he committed suicide.

On the day that proved fatal for von Kluge one French and three American divisions landed at St Tropez on the French Riviera. Meeting little opposition they pushed up the Rhone valley. By 3 September they had captured Lyons and on the 11th they joined forces with Allied troops driving east from Brittany. To the north the shattered German forces streamed back towards their own borders. Along the Loire and Seine the Allied tactical air forces ranged at will, plundering targets of opportunity. In Paris on 25 August, General von Choltitz – disregarding Hitler's orders to destroy the city – surrendered to the 2nd Free French Division under General Leclerc. On the same day De Gaulle entered the city in triumph. He went straight to the Ministry of War, declaring, 'I wished to show that the state ... was returning, first of all, quite simply, to where it belonged.'

On 29 August the last German troops slipped out of a second encirclement and crossed the Seine. They left behind them in Normandy 2,200 destroyed or abandoned armoured vehicles and 210,000 prisoners. Casualties in the fighting had been 240,000 killed and wounded. Three months of fighting in Normandy had cost the Germans twice as many men as at Stalingrad.

The speed of the Allied advance now revealed a fundamental disagreement over strategy among the Allied generals. Eisenhower, who on 1 September had taken over command of the land forces from Montgomery, favoured a broad advance into Germany on all fronts, which would allow Patton's 3rd Army to maintain its impetus towards the Saar on one flank and Montgomery to seize the vital Channel supply ports on the other. Montgomery urged putting all the available resources into a single-pronged thrust by 21st Army Group and US 12th Army Group across Holland and northern Germany to Berlin.

GIs enjoy the fruits of liberation in a Paris café in the spring of 1945.

The liberation of Paris, 25 August 1944.

Eisenhower overruled Montgomery and, juggling his increasingly stretched supply lines, opted for a modified version of the broad front strategy, allowing Montgomery to push Dempsey's British 2nd Army forward with General Hodges' US 1st Army on his right. Patton was told he could move as far as possible on whatever was left over.

The speed of the Allied advance threatened to make the broad front/narrow thrust argument seem academic. Eisenhower confidently expected to capture the Ruhr and Saar by the middle of September. British 2nd Army had entered Brussels on 3 September, its tanks racing over World War I battlefields where men had fought for months for an advantage of a few yards. On the next day General Dempsey captured Antwerp and its port facilities intact. But, crucially, the German 15th Army still held the lower reaches of the Scheldt, which controlled the approaches to Antwerp. Nevertheless, it looked as if German resistance was disintegrating everywhere.

On 4 September Hitler reinstated von Rundstedt as Commander in Chief West. According to his chief of staff, General Westphal, 'Until the middle of October the enemy could have broken through at any point he liked, with ease, and would then have been able to cross the Rhine and thrust deep into Germany almost unhindered.' Along the entire Western front the Germans could muster only 100 serviceable tanks. On 4 September, between the outskirts of Antwerp and the Ruhr there were, according to General Student, 'only recruit and convalescent units and one coast-defence division from Holland. They were reinforced by a panzer detachment of merely 25 tanks and self-propelled guns.'

The crew of an A22 Churchill infantry tank are mobbed by the citizens of Brussels as they drive into the liberated city on 3 September 1944.

At this point the Allies became the victims of their own success. They had now arrived at a point which, when planning the invasion, they had not expected to reach until May 1945. Like the Red Army in April 1944 they had outrun their supplies, which trailed back 350 miles across a war-wracked Europe to the Channel. The continued occupation by the Germans of the Channel and Atlantic ports left Cherbourg as the only large harbour open to the Allies. The Scheldt estuary was not cleared until early November and the first Allied convoy to dock in Antwerp did not arrive until the end of the month. These problems were exacerbated by the Allies' lavish daily requirement of 700 tons of ammunition, equipment and rations for each of their divisions, compared with a German divisional requirement of 200 tons. As Eisenhower later admitted, 'the life blood of supply was running perilously thin throughout the forward extremities of the Army.' On 30 August, as Patton's spearheads

People of the Belgian town of Arras shake their fists at a portrait of Hitler. Arras was liberated by British 2nd Army in its lightning thrust through Belgium to Antwerp.

reached the Moselle, the bulk of his US 3rd Army – already restricted to a mere 32,000 tons of fuel a day instead of the normal 400,000 – came to a grinding halt with the Rhine crossings only 75 miles away. The fuel shortage was compounded by a confusion of competing options. An airborne invasion of Belgium was planned but never carried out, resulting in a week-long interruption of air supplies and the loss of 1.5 million tons of fuel, enough to get all the Allied armies to the Rhine.

With defeat staring them in the face, the Germans were able to regroup. A scarecrow army of 135,000 cadets, lines of communications troops and convalescents set to work rebuilding the West Wall, much of which had been stripped in 1943 to bolster the Atlantic Wall. Like a portly magician producing a rabbit from a hat, Goering revealed the existence of six parachute regiments and a further 10,000 men from redundant Luftwaffe ground and air crew. They became 1st Parachute Army.

In the most vulnerable sector of the front – the northern area leading to the Ruhr – 9th and 10th armoured SS Divisions were refitting near Arnhem. Thus they were in position to frustrate Montgomery's airborne attempt to cross the Rhine – Operation Market Garden – which began on 17 September. Three airborne divisions were dropped with the aim of seizing the bridges on the Eindhoven-Arnhem road in order to enable 2nd Army of 21st Group to outflank the West Wall. The first part of the plan was successful: US 101st Airborne Division, dropped between Veghel and Eindhoven, captured the two southern bridges, and 2nd Army raced to link up with US 82nd Airborne at Grave and Nijmegen. But at Arnhem, the most northerly target, the British 1st Airborne Division ran into trouble. Dropped some eight miles from their objective, they found their way blocked by powerful German forces. Only one British battalion managed to reach the bridge, where it was cut off. The rest of 1st Airborne were forced back into a bridgehead near Oosterbeck and awaited relief. The bridge at Nijmegen was finally cleared on 20 September by 82nd Airborne and British 30th Corps, but when they tried to push on to Arnhem, through a narrow corridor, they were shelled heavily by the Germans from both sides. The weather deteriorated, air support and supply broke down. The Polish Parachute Brigade was sacrificed in a vain bid to break the German ring. Even when 2nd Army arrived, it was only with great difficulty that the survivors of 1st Airborne were evacuated.

By the end of September the Germans had stabilized their front in the west. Taking advantage of their interior lines, they were now able to build up their units at a faster pace than the Allies. The Americans had captured Aachen at the end of October, after three weeks of bitter fighting, but a general offensive in November, launched on a 600-mile front by all the Allied armies, brought little gain at considerable cost. In the north the British were still 30 miles from the Rhine, a distance they were not to cover until the spring of 1945.

THE RED ARMY

On 23 June – the day Herbert Morrison told the British public about the V-1s – the Russians opened their summer offensive against Busch's Army Group Centre in Belorussia, north-west and south-east of Vitebsk. The Red Army was now a very different organization from the one that almost disintegrated in the campaigns of 1941 and 1942. Tens of thousands of American trucks had given it a strategic and tactical mobility superior to the bulk of the Wehrmacht. The ruthless reorganization of 1943 had seen the development of 'operational manoeuvre groups' – highly mobile, élite armoured formations whose task was to flow through the breaches in the enemy lines, smashing up his reserves and lines of communications in the rear areas. The Soviet air force – for two years the punchbag of the Luftwaffe – was now able to strike deeply behind the German fronts in an interdiction role and provide immediate tactical support for the Red Army.

The disasters of 1941 and 1942 had been followed by a marked improvement at both the top and the bottom of the Red Army's command structure. The shake out at the top had left Stalin with a number of able commanders – Zhukov, Konev, Rokossovsky and the brilliant young Chernyakhovsky, tragically killed in action in 1945 at the age of 38 – upon whom he could rely to exercise their own judgement. At the junior level the harsh reality of the battlefield had fostered a growing tactical awareness. It was the middle level which provided the weakest rung of the ladder. Many commanders still went in greater dread of their superiors than of the enemy, often with good reason. During the Polish campaign of 1944 Marshal Zhukov, accompanied by Marshal Konstantin Rokossovsky and General Pavel Bator, was watching an attack on the German lines. Suddenly Zhukov lowered his binoculars and barked, 'The corps commander and the commander of the 44th Rifle Division – penal battalion!' Frantic pleading by Rokossovsky and Bator saved the corps commander's

The SU-152 self-propelled gun, dubbed the 'hunter' by the Red Army. This highly successful weapon was created by mounting a 152mm howitzer on the chassis of the KV-15 heavy tank.

The face of defeat. An infantryman of von Manstein's Army Group South during the German counter-offensive at Zhitomir, west of Kiev, in December 1943.

skin but not the general commanding 44th Rifle Division. He was stripped of his rank on the spot and despatched to lead a suicide attack on the German lines in which he was killed almost instantly. Having served Zhukov's draconian disciplinary purposes, he was posthumously created a Hero of the Soviet Union.

To the end of the war there was an extraordinary contrast between the ruthlessly modernized élite Guards divisions – bristling with tanks, artillery and rocket launchers – and the seemingly inexhaustible mass of infantry who came in their wake, evoking images of the Dark Ages hordes. General von Manteuffel, one of Germany's finest panzer commanders, painted a vivid picture of the advance of the Red Army: 'Behind the tank spearheads rolls on a vast horde, largely mounted on horses. The soldier carries a sack on his back, with dry crusts of bread and raw vegetables collected on the march from the fields and villages. The horses eat the straw from the roofs – they get very little else. The Russians are accustomed to carry on for as long as three weeks in this primitive way, when advancing. You can't stop them, like an ordinary army, by cutting their communications, for you rarely find any supply columns to strike.' As the experienced General von Tippelskirch observed, against such an army one needs forces 'with masterly leadership, first-class training, high morale and excellent nerves'.

Soviet artillery rolls off the production line. The Russian war effort was stiffened by a massive injection of American material. By mid-1943 the United States had shipped in over 900,000 tons of steel and $150 million worth of machine tools. In their wake came 138,000 trucks, and 12,000 tons of butter earmarked for troops convalescing in military hospitals.

THE HAMMER BLOW

Now the Soviet Union was moving out of the 'strategic defensive' phase of the war and was about to take the initiative on all fronts. Stretched over a front of nearly 2,000 miles, the Germans had to guess at the weight, location and direction of the Russian attack. When it came, it fell like a hammer blow on Army Group Centre. Within a week, most of 3rd Panzer Army was destroyed in a battle of annihilation around Vitebsk. Two weeks later 100,000 Germans were encircled at Minsk. By the end of the first week in July it was clear that Army Group Centre was falling apart. Casualties were at least 300,000, and 31 of the 47 German corps and divisional commanders were taken prisoner. As they reeled back under the Russian onslaught the Germans were fast running out of space in which to manoeuvre and allow the Soviet hurricane to blow itself out. They were even more quickly running out of men to replace their grievous losses. The path to the Baltic states and East Prussia now lay open.

'Ivan' – troops typical of the millions of Red Army men who fought the war on the Eastern Front. These horse-drawn anti-tank guns were photographed at the end of their advance, 55 miles west of Berlin, on 8 May 1945.

Busch's successor, Model, managed to extricate the remnants of Army Group Centre, but only by disobeying Hitler's orders to hold every inch of ground to the last man. However, by the end of July Army Group North, covering the Baltic states, was cut off by the Russians and penned inside the Courland peninsula – a province of Latvia surrounded on three sides by the Baltic. Hitler refused to sanction a break-out and there its 22 divisions, meaninglessly redesignated Army Group Courland, stayed to the end of the war, while Germany bled to death on all fronts, a monument to the Fuehrer's bankrupt strategy.

In five weeks the Red Army advanced 400 miles, bringing them exhausted and at the end of their supply lines to the outskirts of Warsaw. On 1 August the Polish Home Army in that city rose against the German garrison. The Russians remained halted on their bridgeheads on the east bank of the Vistula while the fighting raged inside Warsaw. The Western Allies requested air landing facilities on Soviet soil to attempt to supply the Poles with arms and medical supplies. The Russians refused, a hint of the Cold War waiting in the wings. On 2 October the resistance inside Warsaw came to an end. Nearly 200,000 civilians had died and thousands more were deported to Germany. Polish impetuosity and icy Russian calculation had combined to create the tragedy in Warsaw. After the experience of Stalingrad the Russians needed no reminding of the hideous cost of taking a city street by street. Even while the Poles fought inside Warsaw, outside the Red Army lost 123,000 troops to determined German counter-attacks and in the final drive into the Polish capital. The battles for Budapest and Berlin were still to come. Even if Marshal Rokossovsky had fought his way into Warsaw during August, he

'Ruined Warsaw', painted by the artist Julius B. Stafford Baker.

A German assault gun noses its way through the streets of Warsaw in August 1944.

would then have been faced with a well-organized patriotic army, 35,000 strong, who were as anti-Soviet as they were anti-German. The Russians would have dealt with them but at this stage in the war Stalin was unwilling to risk an open confrontation with the British and Americans over Poland. He let the Germans do his work for him.

Even after the Warsaw uprising was crushed, the Red Army concentrated on clearing its flanks in the Baltic and the Balkans. By the end of October the Russians had established a firm foothold in East Prussia. In the south they struck at Rumania on 20 August. Three days later its pro-German fascist leader Marshal Antonescu was overthrown. In the sweltering heat and billowing dust of high summer the German 6th Army was encircled. Divisional commanders had to glean the intelligence by listening to the sounds of battle around them and by visiting their neighbours, if they could be found. While Hitler pondered the retrieval of an already hopeless situation with a bombing raid on Bucharest, the Russians raced on to seize the Rumanian capital on 31 August. Next Bulgaria was invaded and quickly occupied. The Bulgarians then declared war on Germany, and their armed forces, about 500,000 strong, were taken under Soviet command and used, together with purged Rumanian formations, to continue the war in the Balkans.

Six days after entering Bucharest the Red Army crossed the Yugoslav border, where it pivoted northwards in a massive flanking manoeuvre to roll up the exposed south-eastern flank in Hungary, the strategic centre of Europe. Red Army units penetrated the suburbs of Budapest at the end of October, but it was not until the middle of February 1945 that the city – stubbornly defended by four divisions – fell into Russian hands. Nevertheless, in the autumn of 1944 Stalin had achieved his object – he had placed the countries of the Balkans under Soviet control and prevented them from going over to the Western Allies, as might have happened if German occupation had been ended by the sudden collapse of the Third Reich rather than by Soviet military victory. Thus was Germany saved for another six months.

THE LAST THROW

In East Prussia Hitler had chosen to abandon personally his doctrine of 'no withdrawal'. In November he left Rastenburg for the last time. Brooding over the maps in the 'Wolf's Lair', Hitler's gambler's eye had spotted an opportunity for one last counterstroke in the west.

The Americans and the British were still infected with the over-confidence which stemmed from the easy victories of the late summer. Montgomery was looking forward to a spot of Christmas leave. He told his troops in mid-December, 'The enemy is at present fighting a defensive campaign on all fronts: his situation is that he cannot stage major offensive operations.' Everyone thought that the Germans were finished.

Like the hapless General Gamelin four years before, Eisenhower had left the Ardennes sector thinly defended – only six divisions on a 70-mile front. Here, where he had settled the fate of France in a single afternoon, Hitler planned to repeat the triumphs of June 1940. A quick victory was necessary, the Fuehrer argued, 'before the French should begin to conscript their manpower'. It was as if, in Hitler's mind, the war would go on for ever and that after five years he had merely come back to square one, ready for the second round. Once again German armies would drive through the forests of the Ardennes to the Meuse, then sweep north to capture the port of Antwerp. Cut off from their supply bases, the British would be forced into a second Dunkirk. The 'artificial' coalition would fall apart 'with a tremendous thunderclap' and Germany would turn to deal with the threat from the east.

It was the last of Hitler's intuitive masterstrokes, the last occasion on which that inveterate gambler still possessed enough chips to double the stakes. It was a bold plan, sweeping in concept, and impossible to execute. When on 24 October von Rundstedt was presented with the plan, 'I was staggered ... It was obvious to me that the available forces were far too small – In fact no soldier really believed that the aim of reaching Antwerp was really practicable. But I knew by now it was useless to protest to Hitler about the *possibility* of anything.'

Hitler brushed aside von Rundstedt's suggestion that the offensive

Soviet infantrymen move into action on the outskirts of Budapest, January 1945.

German shock troops advance at the start of the Ardennes offensive, 17 December 1944.

Exhaustion shows on the faces of men of the 110th Regiment, US 28th Infantry Division, after two days of heavy fighting for the Clef crossings which denied the vital road centre of Bastogne to von Manteuffel's 5th Panzer Army at the start of the Ardennes offensive.

should be scaled down to a more modest attempt to pinch out the American forces which had pushed beyond Aachen as far as the River Roer. In conditions of the greatest secrecy the plans were drawn up, with Hitler controlling every detail, right down to the daily decisions as to the supply of vehicles and horses to the individual divisions making up the attack forces. When von Rundstedt received the final orders, the words 'Not To Be Altered' were scrawled across them in Hitler's spidery hand. Thoroughly disgusted, von Rundstedt relinquished the overall control of operations to Model and spent the better part of the offensive drinking brandy.

The attack went in at 5.30am on 16 December. The Germans committed 28 divisions to the battle (in 1940 the advance through the Ardennes to the Channel had been launched by 44 divisions, which had risen to 71 by the time it had reached its objective). After a 20-minute barrage hundreds of searchlights flickered on, creating 'artificial moonlight'. Moments later German shock troops emerged from the thick winter mists, overwhelming the dazed Americans in the front line. In the American rear areas German infiltrators, dressed in American uniform, cut telephone wires and spread confusion. At first there was something approaching blind panic behind the American lines. At Manderfeld, HQ of US 14th Cavalry Group and now directly in the path of von Manteuffel's 5th Panzer Army, staff officers completely lost their nerve. They fled in their vehicles and, in a desperate attempt to dispose of anything which might aid the Germans, simply set the whole town ablaze. The opening drive shattered two American divisions spread along the Schnee Eifel ridge

M4A3E8 Shermans drawn up during the fighting in the Ardennes, January 1945.

in the north and along the River Our in the south. Scattered fragments of these divisions wandered about the wintry forest, fighting the Germans when they collided with them, or trying to link up with larger formations.

After four days of confused fighting, the Americans pulled themselves together. On the north 'shoulder' of the German advance General Gerow blocked Sepp Dietrich's 6th SS Panzer Army. The 101st Airborne Division clung on grimly to the vital road centre of Bastogne, forcing von Manteuffel to bypass it as he pressed on to the Meuse. The Germans were now rapidly running out of time and fuel – they had begun the offensive with only a quarter of their minimum petrol requirement. As they fell back the Americans fired their fuel dumps. In the south Patton wheeled his entire front through 90 degrees and drove on Bastogne. In order to prevent the expanding German salient from severing Bradley's communications with his troops on the northern side of the 'Bulge', Eisenhower gave Montgomery temporary overall command in the north. Montgomery was still smarting from the rejection of his 'narrow thrust' strategy. With his usual sublime lack of tact he could not resist the opportunity to 'tweak our Yankee noses', as Bradley put it. One of his own staff officers recalled that Montgomery had arrived at the headquarters of General Hodges' US 1st Army like 'Christ come to cleanse the temple'. (After the battle Monty made things worse at a press conference by claiming virtually the entire credit for the eventual victory – 'The battle has been most interesting. I think possibly one of the most tricky ... I have ever handled'. Churchill was obliged to mollify the outraged Americans with a generous speech in the House of Commons.)

On Christmas Eve von Manteuffel's most advanced units were fought to a halt by US 2nd Armoured Division just three miles short of

below right A reconnaissance squadron of General Collins' US 7th Corps in a brush with snipers on the northern edge of the Ardennes 'bulge' in the first week of January 1945.

the Meuse. Two days later Bastogne was relieved by US 4th Armoured Division. As early as 22 December, von Rundstedt – mindful of the growing threat on the Eastern Front – had begged Hitler to call off the offensive. The Fuehrer ordered his commanders to slog on and, on 1 January, launched a second, abortive, attack southwards from the Saar. By now the mist which had masked the initial German thrust had lifted and the Allied air forces ranged over the battlefield. On the morning of the 29th, the tank commander Major-General von Mellenthin set off for 9th Panzer Division: 'the icebound roads glittered in the sunshine and I witnessed the uninterrupted air attacks on our traffic routes and supply dumps. Not a single German plane was in the air, innumerable vehicles were shot up and their blackened wrecks littered the roads.'

The American counterattacks went in on 3 January and by the end of the month the last vestige of the German salient in the Ardennes had disappeared. The Germans had lost 100,000 men and 800 tanks, roughly the same number as the Americans. The Americans made good their losses in a fortnight. The Germans never recovered. In the battle of the Bulge Hitler had squandered the last remaining reserves of strength in the German army.

DWINDLING RESOURCES

One of the principal causes of the breakdown of the Ardennes offensive was the Allied air forces' destruction of German oil resources. By the end of 1944 the German war economy had slipped out of control, presenting a picture of absurd contrasts. In September 1944, 3,000 fighters rolled out of the war factories. In the same month aviation spirit production fell to a mere 10,000 tons, measured against the Luftwaffe's April consumption of 165,000 tons. The planes stood on the runway with empty fuel tanks and empty cockpits, as the training of pilots had virtually broken down. Under Armaments Minister Albert Speer's assiduous direction, armoured vehicle production reached a peak in December 1944, but by then the offensive against the German transport system had destroyed nearly half of its marshalling capacity. Of the combined total of 2,199 tanks produced in September-November 1944, only 1,372 reached the troops, to replace 1,575 lost in the fighting. This surge in production, combined

Men of the *Volkssturm* shoulder arms. The man in the middle of the rear line is carrying a *Panzerfaust* on his shoulder. This was a robust and highly effective single-shot projector for a grenade capable of penetrating 140mm of armour plate. By the end of the war improvements had increased the weapon's range from 30m to 150m.

with the loss of raw materials and resources from the territories overrun by the Russians, served only to hasten the final collapse.

In the field the German army was still just over five million strong, but it was burning away at the core. In 1944, 106 divisions were destroyed, three more than had been mobilized in September 1939.

Boy soldiers of the Third Reich.

Hitler insisted on replacing each one of these with new divisions rather than use the replacements to bolster existing units. Albert Speer gloomily observed, 'New divisions were formed in great numbers, equipped with new weapons and sent to the front without any experience or training, while at the same time the good, battle-hardened units bled to death because they were given no replacement weapons or personnel.'

The constant drain on manpower called for desperate measures. Conscription was extended to bring in sixteen- and fifty-year-olds. Military hospitals were trawled for convalescing soldiers strong enough to hold a rifle. They were drafted into the ironically named 'stomach' and 'ear' battalions, made up entirely of men suffering from stomach complaints or defective hearing. The autumn of 1944 saw the introduction, under Himmler's direction, of the *Volksgrenadier* divisions, scraped together from replacement units, shattered divisions and depot staffs. They were of little military value, and their inexperience proved disastrous when they were committed to battle in the Ardennes offensive.

Grandiose names masked a weakness which might have provoked a smile were it not so tragic. In January 1945 Hitler ordered the formation of a 'tank-destroyer division'. In reality this formation consisted of bicycle companies equipped with anti-tank grenades.

A WORLD IN FLAMES

Just as 'Dad's Army' might have cycled off in the summer sunshine to tackle Pzkpfw Mk IVs if the Germans had crossed the Channel in 1940, so the men of the 'tank-destroyer' division wheeled their way eastward to take on the Red Army's T-34s in the snow and sleet of mid-winter 1945.

The idea of a German Home Guard had been suggested initially by Heusinger, Chief of the General Staff Operations Branch, and had been turned down by Hitler. But with the breaching of the Reich's frontiers some form of civilian defence was thought necessary. The *Volkssturm* was established on 25 September 1944. All males between the ages of 16 and 60 not in the armed services but capable of bearing arms were to be conscripted into its ranks. Inevitably the *Volkssturm* fell foul of the competing fiefdoms in Germany's chaotic power structure. It came under the command not of the Army but of the Nazi Party. Guderian recalled the unhappy results: 'the brave men of the *Volkssturm* … were in many cases drilled busily in the proper way of giving the Hitler salute instead of being trained in the use of weapons, of which they had no previous experience.' Finally, on 28 January 1945, Hitler ordered that, whenever possible, units of the *Volkssturm* should be combined in the field with troops of the regular army. Thus would the *Volkssturm* receive 'stiffening and support'.

Bicycle-borne troops set out for the front armed with *Panzerfaust* weapons.

RETURN TO BERLIN

Hitler returned to Berlin from the west on 16 January. At first he took up residence in the Reich Chancellery. The new Chancellery building had been designed as the starting point for the rebuilding of Berlin. Now, pounded and pockmarked by bomb blasts, it loomed like a great grey hulk in a sea of destruction. Its boarded-up windows gazed sightlessly out on to a moonscape of craters and rubble. In the last four months of the war Berlin was under almost constant aerial bombardment, from American B-17s by day and RAF Mosquitoes by night. By the end of the war three billion cubic feet of debris carpeted the streets, enough rubble for a mountain more than a thousand feet high. Every third house had been destroyed or rendered uninhabitable. In the area round the Chancellery the destruction was

Australian bomber crews celebrate a Lancaster's 100th mission. The aircraft displays a redundant boast by Hermann Goering. In the autumn of 1944 the strategic air offensive moved towards its climax – during this period Bomber Command alone dropped more bombs on Germany than it had during the entire course of 1943.

85 per cent. After each raid a pall of black dust hung over the city before drifting down to form a slimy sediment over its shattered streets and buildings.

Evacuation, war casualties and the call-up of men and women had reduced Berlin's population by over a third. The bulk of the male population was either under 16 or over 60. Yet in the midst of devastation Berliners strove to preserve the vestiges of normality. Twelve thousand policemen stayed at their posts. The mail continued to be delivered, right up to the last few days of the war. While the *Volkssturm* fought the Red Army in one street letters were being delivered in the next. The telephones still functioned, as did the underground and overhead railways. Even a section of Berlin's famous zoo remained open to visitors. The Berlin Philharmonic's season ran on until the end of March.

Workers rose at dawn to negotiate the masonry-choked streets to their factories, 65 per cent of which were still in some kind of working condition. Working alongside them were Berlin's 100,000 slave labourers, a fraction of the seven million people imported from the conquered territories and put to work in Germany's industry, business and homes. Even the War Ministry in the Bendlerstrasse had a large contingent of foreign workers. As the end drew near, many of the slave labourers were directed to prepare the defences of Berlin. Lance-Corporal Norman Norris, a British POW being marched through Berlin in April noted, 'Huge tank traps were now being dug, one at Koenigswarterhausen by Polish jews. They looked plaintively at us; the look in their eyes showing that they knew they would eventually be murdered was unforgettable.'

A WORLD IN FLAMES
THE BUNKER

Few Berliners knew that Hitler had returned to the capital. At first he moved into his quarters in a section of the Chancellery which remained undamaged by the bombing. The window panes were intact and thick grey curtains shut out the dismal scene outside. Hitler rarely ventured beyond the Chancellery, but shortly after his return to Berlin he drove out to Goebbels' home to take tea, an indication that the Propaganda Minister had been restored to favour. Hitler spent most of the afternoon reminiscing with Goebbels over the heady days of 1932 and the plans for the rebuilding of Berlin, themes which were to be endlessly recapitulated in the days to come. But pulsing away behind these recollections of the days of power and fantasies of reconstruction was the nihilism which lay at the heart of Hitler's philosophy – world power or ruin. World power had, fleetingly, seemed within his grasp when his armies reached out for Moscow. Now ruin stared him in the face, releasing an abstract mania for destruction, a gleeful rush to catastrophe. In 1939 Hitler had quivered

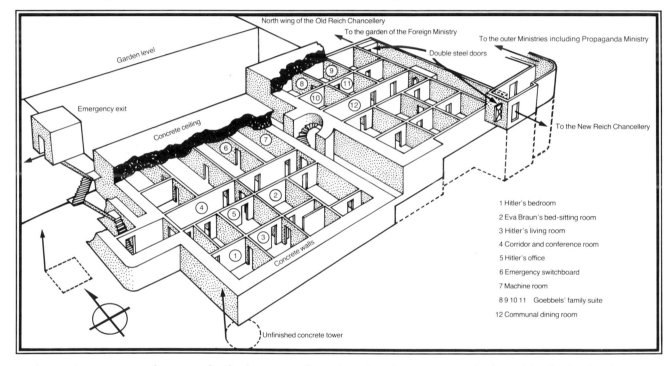

with excitement as he watched the merciless bombardment of Warsaw. In 1941 he ordered the annihilation of Leningrad, and three years later painted voluptuous pictures to his generals of a London pulverized beyond recognition by flying bombs. In the 1930s Hitler had promised that if Germany were to lose the coming war, 'even as we go down to destruction we will carry half the world into destruction with us.' Now Goebbels was to be his confidant and stage manager in the operatic orchestration of the strategy of doom. In a permanent revolution of destruction lay the only hope of survival. As the bombs rained down on Berlin, Goebbels threw himself into his task, exulting, 'The bomb terror spares the dwellings of neither rich nor poor; before the labour offices of total war the last class barriers go down.' Chaos was to be embraced as the necessary preliminary to the New Order: 'Now the bombs, instead of killing all Europeans, have only smashed the prison walls which held them captive … In trying to destroy Europe's future, the enemy has only succeeded in smashing its past; and with that, everything old and outworn has gone.'

A plan of the Berlin Bunker

On 30 January, Hitler delivered his last speech over the radio. In flat, weary tones he told the German people, 'However grave the crisis may be at the moment, in the end it will be mastered by our unalterable will, by our readiness for sacrifice and by our abilities. We will overcome this emergency also.' As the bombing increased in intensity, he spent more and more time in the concrete shelter built in the Chancellery garden. Eventually he moved underground permanently, in what became the 13th and last FHQ, part tinny echo of the caves of the Niebelungen, part throwback to the dug-outs in which Corporal Hitler sheltered in the First World War.

Extending beneath the Chancellery garden, the Bunker was part of an elaborate complex of shelters, one of which housed Martin Bormann, Head of the Party Chancery, his staff and various service chiefs, and another SS Brigadefuehrer Mohnke, the commandant of the Chancellery. Buried 55 feet below the ground, the Bunker was built in two storeys, with exterior walls six feet thick and an eight-foot-thick concrete canopy on top of which was piled 30 feet of earth. In the Bunker's upper level were the kitchen, staff living quarters and, towards the end, rooms for Goebbels' family. Connected to the upper bunker by a short spiral staircase was the Fuehrerbunker proper, divided into 18 cramped, low-ceilinged rooms grouped on either side of a central passageway. Daily conferences were held in the passageway, which was closed off for the purpose by a partition. To the right of the passageway were rooms occupied by Goebbels and the SS physician Dr Stumpfegger. To the left was a suite of six rooms occupied by Hitler. The small living room – 10 feet by 15 – was dominated by Anton Graff's oil painting of Frederick the Great. Hitler had purchased the portrait in Munich in 1934 and it was the one item of furniture which had followed him to all the previous FHQs. In the Bunker he would spend long lonely hours brooding over the image of the soldier-king. On one occasion the valet Sergeant Roschus Misch accidentally broke in one one of these reveries: 'It was very late, and I thought that the Fuehrer had already retired ... There was Der Chef, gazing at the picture by candlelight. He was sitting there, motionless, his chin buried in his hand, as if he were in a trance. The king seemed to be staring right back. I had barged in, but Hitler took no notice of me. So I tiptoed out. It was like stumbling on someone at prayer.'

The airless claustrophobia of this concrete cave was the final bleak expression of the artificiality and isolation of Hitler's own existence. In the baleful glare of electric lights night merged into day. The last military conference usually ended at 6am, after which Hitler would slump exhausted on to his sofa, seeking relief in plate after plate of cream cakes. In the hours of darkness he would occasionally emerge from the Bunker to take his Alsatian dog Blondi for a short walk through the rubbish-strewn paths of the Chancellery garden, the SS guards hovering at a discreet distance.

In the summer of 1942 the Fuehrer sat at the centre of a vast communications web stretching from the Atlantic coast to the Caucasus. Now his links with the outside world had dwindled to a switchboard of the size required to run a modest hotel, one radio transmitter and one radio-telephone link with the OKW headquarters at Zossen, 15 miles south of Berlin. Much pressure had been put on Hitler by General Jodl and Field Marshal Keitel, Commander-in-Chief of the Combined Forces (Wehrmacht), to move his headquarters to Zossen. Hitler expressed his doubts about the soundness of 'army concrete'. In the Bunker, surrounded by his SS guards, he remained

safe to draft the script of his own end in the fires of Berlin, not some
obscure Mark of Brandenburg hamlet. His commanders would have to
come to him, a process greatly facilitated by the shrinking perimeter
defended by his armies*.

Those who made the trip to the Bunker were left with an indelible
impression of its suffocating atmosphere, pregnant with fear and
suppressed hysteria. Captain Beermann, one of the SS guard,
recalled the debilitating effects of long spells spent in the Bunker: 'It
was like being stranded in a cement submarine, or buried down in
some charnel house. People who work in diving bells probably feel
less cramped. It was both dark and dusty, for some of the cement was
old, some new. In the long hours of the night, it would be deathly
silent, except for the hum of the generator. When you came upon flesh
and blood people their faces seemed blanched in the artificial light.
The ventilation could now be warm and sultry, now cold and clammy.
The walls were sometimes grey, some bleached orange; some were
moist and even mouldy ... Then there was the fetid odour of boots,
sweaty woollen uniforms, acrid coal-tar disinfectant. Towards the
end, when the drainage packed up, it was as pleasant as working in a
public urinal.'

To all those who saw him, Hitler presented a dreadful physical
spectacle, like a man risen from the grave. Awash with the drugs
provided by the 'Reich Injection Master' Dr Morell; hunched and

*Hitler made his last trip to the front in March, driving in a Volkswagen to the
castle at Freienwalde to confer with generals and staff of 9th Army.

shaking, with faltering voice and glaucous eyes, a crust of spittle and cake crumbs flecking his lips, his jacket blotched with food stains. Captain Gerhard Boldt saw the Fuehrer for the first time when he attended a briefing in the Bunker early in February: 'His head was slightly wobbling. His left arm hung slackly and his hand trembled a good deal. There was an indescribable flickering light in his eye, creating a fearsome and wholly unnatural effect. His face and the parts around his eyes gave the impression of total exhaustion. All his movements were those of a senile man.'

Despite his physical disintegration Hitler still retained the power to excite those who came to see him with the wildest of hopes. In the middle of March the distraught Gauleiter of Danzig arrived in the Bunker. Over a thousand Russian tanks were at the gates of the city, he wailed, with only four Tigers to oppose them. He declared that he was determined to present Hitler with 'the whole frightful reality of the situation'. But after a brief audience he emerged 'completely transformed'. The Fuehrer had promised 'new divisions' – Danzig would be saved. Only Albert Speer had the courage and the detachment to overcome the overpowering ties of loyalty and contemplate killing Hitler and bringing the whole grisly charade to an end. He planned to flood the Bunker's ventilation system with poison gas, but the quite coincidental covering of the air intake with a tall metal chimney thwarted his plans.

THE HOUSE OF CARDS

On 9 January General Guderian warned the Fuehrer 'the Eastern Front is like a pack of cards'. Hitler dismissed Guderian's figures on the strength of the Russian forces deployed along the Vistula and the East Prussian border as 'the greatest bluff since Genghis Khan'. For the drive into Germany along the Warsaw-Berlin axis the Stavka had assembled an army of appropriate proportions. To the south of Warsaw, Zhukov's 1st Belorussian and Marshal Konev's 1st Ukrainian Fronts disposed of 163 rifle divisions, 32,143 guns and heavy mortars, 6,500 tanks and 4,772 aircraft. The Red Army enjoyed a 5:1 advantage in manpower and armour; a 7:1 advantage in artillery and – a mark of the eclipse of the Luftwaffe – a 17:1 advantage in aircraft. Along a front which stretched 300 miles there were 64 guns and 12 tanks to each kilometre.

The offensive was opened in the swirling snowstorms of 12 January. Hitler's Vistula front was torn to pieces in a matter of days. Warsaw was encircled by 47th Army and fell on 17th January. Lodz and Cracow fell on the 19th, and 24 hours later Zhukov's advanced columns – racing over the frozen ground – were pressing on across the Silesian border. On 31 January they reached the Oder. The tip of the salient which Zhukov had driven into eastern Germany like a giant snowplough was now at Küstrin, only 48 miles from Berlin. On 26 January Zhukov had submitted plans to the Stavka for an all-out assault on Berlin. But the threat to his communications posed by the encircled but unreduced garrisons in Poznan, Glogau and Breslau, and the possibility of a German counter-attack on his exposed flanks, forced him to call a halt. While the Russians hesitated General Wenck launched a limited counter-offensive – codenamed *Sonnenwende* (Solstice) – on Zhukov's right flank. *Sonnenwende* made hardly a dent in the 1st Belorussian Front's deployment. Nevertheless, it had a quite disproportionate effect, confirming the Russians in their caution. On 17 February the Stavka turned Zhukov away from Berlin and directed him to clear the east bank of the Oder.

A formation of USAAF B-17 Flying Fortresses of 381st Group with a P51 Mustang escort in the background. Powered by a Rolls Royce Merlin engine and fitted with a long-range drop tank, the Mustangs were able to escort the bombers all the way to their targets in Germany whilst at the same time outperforming all the German fighters and effectively driving the Luftwaffe from the skies.

A WORLD IN FLAMES

AN ELEPHANT LEANING ON A HOUSE

On 8 February the final Allied offensive in the west opened with an attack by Canadian 1st Army on the Reichswald forest, in the angle between the Rhine and the Dutch frontier. The battle recalled Passchendaele – a massive artillery bombardment followed by a bloody slugging match in the flooded countryside, where every yard was bitterly contested by 1st Parachute Army. This was the first in a series of ponderous blows struck along Eisenhower's 'broad front' down the Rhine from Nijmegen to the Moselle. There was little strategic subtlety in the approach – it was like an elephant leaning on a frame house – but sheer weight of numbers, and the skilful tactical combination of all arms, made it effective. On 3 March Canadian 1st Army joined hands with US 9th Army at Geldern and within a week the last German bridgehead west of the Rhine in this sector, opposite Wessel, had disappeared. By 6 March US 1st Army was in Cologne. In the south Patton was driving through the Palatinate, linking up with General Patch's US 7th Army to surround most of Hausser's Army Group G.

German prisoners of war are marched through the 'Dragon's teeth' of the Siegfried line.

German resistance west of the Rhine was now falling apart and they set about denying the Rhine bridges to the Americans. On the evening of 2 March an American tank column reached the Rhine opposite Düsseldorf, only to be greeted by the sight of the bridge at Obersachsel collapsing into the river. Twelve more bridges were successfully blown by the Germans in the following five days, forcing the Americans to go back to their plans for an amphibious crossing.

Twenty-five miles upstream from Bonn is the town of Remagen. When advance units of the US 9th Armoured Division entered the town on the afternoon of 7 March, they were astonished to discover that the Ludendorff railway bridge was still standing, defended only by a handful of engineers and teenage members of the *Volkssturm*. In the autumn of 1918, Ludendorff's nerve had finally cracked, but the bridge named after him held firm when two charges failed to forestall the Americans as they raced to capture the prize. The main charge failed to go off, and 9th Armoured had secured a bridgehead on the Rhine.

Hitler immediately ordered a counter-attack, but his obsession with defending the *west* bank of the Rhine had denuded the defences on

The border city of Aachen fell to US 1st Army only after particularly bitter fighting. Head bowed, the commander of the German garrison is driven away into captivity in the front seat of an American jeep.

the east bank. It took two days for 11th Panzer Grenadiers Division to arrive on the scene, by which time US 1st Army had moved three divisions across the river and was expanding the bridgehead by the hour. In a last, desperate attempt to retrieve the situation, the Luftwaffe sent in 20 aircraft to bomb the bridge. They lost five of their planes and scored three hits. Their task was finished by artillery fire, but by then American engineers had succeeded in laying three temporary spans alongside. Hitler's retribution was swift. The major who had failed to blow the bridge was shot. Von Rundstedt was sacked as Commander in Chief West and replaced by Kesselring, who greeted his staff with the remark, 'Well, gentlemen, I am the new V-3'.

Civilians pick their way through the rubble of Aachen.

A shell hole in a roof makes a convenient firing position for a British sniper, 12 February 1945.

The capture of the bridge at Remagen threw Eisenhower's plans off balance. Weeks before, it had been agreed that Montgomery was to make the main thrust over the Rhine in the north. Eisenhower put four divisions into the Remagen bridgehead and told them to hang on. While the whole German defence on the lower Rhine crumbled away, everything in this sector went into suspended animation until Montgomery had executed his elaborate set-piece crossing. On the middle Rhine, Patton beat Monty to it by 24 hours. On the night of 22/23 March, General Patton's US 3rd Army took the Rhine at a run south of Mainz at Nierstein. South Germany lay before him – Hitler's futile attempts to block the Allied advance west of the Rhine had cost him a quarter of a million men. Twenty-four hours later, Montgomery's 21st Army Group opened an attack to cross the lower Rhine. Codenamed Operation Plunder, it was planned with all of Montgomery's rigorous attention to detail – in stark contrast to Patton's opportunistic dash. By 23 March 2nd Army's roadhead had received 60,000 tons of ammunition and 30,000 tons of engineering stores alone. In the week preceding the start of operations, movements in the 2nd Army area involved over 6,000 tanks, 4,000 tank transporters and 32,000 wheeled vehicles. The preparations for execution of the crossings absorbed the efforts of nearly 60,000 British and American engineers.

Crossings were made at four points between Rees and a point south of Wessel. An air umbrella was maintained over the bridgehead by nearly 1,000 fighters. An immense artillery barrage prepared the way for an airdrop of 40,000 paratroopers into the battle area to link up with British infantry. They were flown in by over 1,700 aircraft and 1,300 gliders, an awesome demonstration of Allied air power. Immediately following the glider landings, a low-level resupply mission was flown

opposite page War artist Edward Ardizzone's view of two familiar scenes as the Allies pushed on into Germany. White flags of surrender in a small village, and frantic attempts to save precious livestock from the depredations of the military.

by 250 Liberators of 8th US Air Force. On 25 March 1st Army broke out of the bridgehead at Remagen, advancing over six miles. At the same time 21st Army Group established a floating bridge across the Rhine.

The last great concentration of German troops in the west was Model's Army Group B in the Ruhr. The region's industrial importance had already been much reduced by Allied bombing. By the end of March, Bomber Command and the USAAF had systematically sealed off the Ruhr from the rest of Germany, cutting nearly all the communications running eastwards back into the Reich. On the morning of 1 April US units of 1st and 9th Armies met at Paderborn, completing the encirclement of 320,000 German troops. Major-General von Mellenthin witnessed the death throes of Model's army group: 'The greater part of Army Group B was now pent up between the Ruhr and the Sieg, and the circumstances could not have been more depressing. The fog and cold of winter still hung over the land, and the gaunt and broken cities of the Ruhr formed a fitting background to the last act of this tragedy. The great heaps of coal and slag, the shattered buildings, the twisted railway tracks, the ruined bridges, all made their contribution to the gloomy scene. I have seen many battlefields, but none so strange as the great industrial complex of the Ruhr during the final dissolution of Army Group B.'

Model was in a desperate position: not only was he encircled but he also had to grapple with the implications of Hitler's 'scorched-earth' directive of 19th March to destroy all communications, installations, factories and supplies in the path of the enemy. Hitler had told Albert Speer 'If the war is to be lost, the nation also will perish.' Before the encirclement Speer had toured the region, mobilizing his technocrats

right Men of 89th Division US 3rd Army crossing the Rhine at Oberwessel, 26 March 1945.

left The Ludendorff railway bridge photographed from the east bank of the Rhine at 11am on 17 March. Four hours later the bridge finally collapsed. In the left foreground are two M8 light armoured cars.

right Guarding a bridge site across the Rhine.

below An aerial view of the work undertaken by engineers of US 3rd Army during the crossing of the Rhine at Mainz, 7 April 1945.

to defy the order. Model also played his part, limiting himself to purely military demolitions. Fresh 'scorched-earth' instructions streamed westwards from the Fuehrerbunker, but now they bore no relation to reality. On 18 April the Germans in the Ruhr pocket surrendered. In despair Model committed suicide.

THE RACE TO BERLIN

The sudden collapse of German resistance in the West had once again opened up the question of Berlin. In the autumn of 1944 the Allies had decided to make the German capital their target. However, by the end of January Berlin had dropped out of their calculations as a military objective. While the Allies were held up by the Ardennes offensive, the Red Army had forged on to within 50 miles of Berlin. They were now so close they could take it whenever they decided to make the effort. Nevertheless, Churchill still saw Berlin as a prime *political* target, arguing that if the Russians took the city, 'will not their impression that they have been the overwhelming contributors

above Vehicles of US 7th Army roll across the 'Alexander Patch' heavy pontoon bridge built at Worms by the 85th Engineering Corps, 31 March 1945.

German civilians take refuge in a mine in the sector of General Simpson's US 9th Army.

A self-propelled howitzer of 4th Armoured Division US 3rd Army grinds past a grim warning at Worms, 20 March.

to our common victory be unduly imprinted on their minds and may not this lead into a mood which will raise grave and fundamental difficulties in the future?'

The decision was left to Eisenhower, who was reluctant to sustain heavy casualties in racing the Red Army to a city which the Yalta agreements had already placed in the centre of the Soviet postwar occupation zone. In any event, he had uncovered another objective, the 'National Redoubt', a last-ditch stronghold in Bavaria which was being prepared by diehard Nazis. The Redoubt was a chimera, but it exercised a persuasive influence over Eisenhower. On 28 March he cabled Stalin proposing a Soviet-American link-up not in Berlin but 100 miles south in the Leipzig-Dresden area. Later General Bradley wrote, 'The National Redoubt existed largely in the imaginations of a few fanatical Nazis. It grew into so exaggerated a scheme that I am astonished we could have believed it as innocently as we did. But while it persisted this legend ... shaped our tactical thinking.'

A German civilian waving a white flag of surrender approaches an American half-track of US 7th Army on the outskirts of Geisselhardt, 17 April. Diehard Nazis often took savage reprisals against civilian officials who attempted to surrender their towns to the British and Americans. At Lemgo the local burgermeister drove through the German lines in an effort to surrender the town, only to be arrested and shot on the orders of the local military commander, Major-General Paul Goerbig.

Stalin was unimpressed by Eisenhower's message. At a meeting in the Kremlin on 1 April he asked his two rival Marshals, Zhukov and Konev, *'Tak kto zhe budet brat Berlin, my ili soyuzniki?'* ('Well now, who is going to take Berlin, will we or the "little" allies?'). Stalin organized his own race. Zhukov's 1st Belorussian Front was to advance directly west towards the city. Konev's 1st Ukrainian Front was to advance south of a line drawn on the map by Stalin which enabled him to pivot northwards to Berlin after the taking of Lüben, 40 miles from the German capital. For the last battle the Red Army prepared to put into the field 2,000,000 men, 41,600 guns, 6,300 tanks and 7,600 aircraft.

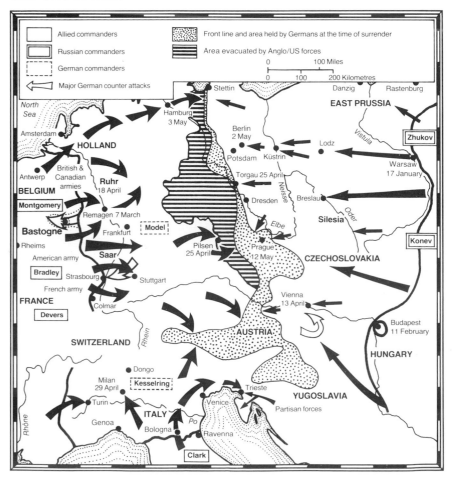

The last stages of the war in Europe.

THE EMPEROR WITHOUT HIS CLOTHES

In the Fuehrerbunker, Hitler's palsied hands still twitched over maps flagged with imaginary armies. His empire had contracted to a narrow corridor in the heart of Germany little more than 100 miles wide. The last German offensive of the war, Operation *Frühlingserwachen*, had been launched in western Hungary early in March. Obsessed with retaining Hungary's Lake Balaton oil fields, Hitler ordered General Wohler's Army Group South to strike towards Budapest and Baja, holding a line along the Danube, while 2nd Panzer Army drove south of Lake Balaton and headed directly east towards the Danube. In the vanguard of the attack was 6th Panzer Army, burning to redeem itself after the failure in the Ardennes and equipped with the PzKpfw VI Tiger II – the 'King Tiger' – massively armoured and mounting an 88mm gun. It was the last fling of Hitler's panzer armies. At the limit of the German advance more than 600 tanks and self-propelled guns tried to batter their way through the Soviet lines south of Lake Velencze. By 15 March it was all over. Hundreds of tanks were left stranded like beached whales in the waterlogged plains of central Hungary. Panzer commanders sourly remarked that they should have been issued with Hitler's new Schnorchel U-boats rather than 'King Tigers', which ploughed to a halt – their fuel tanks empty – to be pounded by Soviet artillery and aircraft. The Red Army counter-offensive swept past their gutted hulks and on to Vienna, which fell on 14 April. The Waffen SS now joined the long list of those who had let down the Fuehrer. Sepp Dietrich's élite units were subjected to the indignity of being stripped of their armband with its embroidered divisional name.

For a brief moment hopes were raised by the death of Roosevelt on 12 April. Now, surely, the alliance would collapse, saving Hitler just as Frederick the Great had been saved by the death of Tsarina Elizabeth. Goebbels, who had been reading aloud to Hitler extracts

below M10 tank destroyers and infantrymen of 30th Division US 9th Army move through the streets of Magdeburg shortly after its capture on 18 April.

below right The despair of teenage German soldiers captured at Nuremberg on 21 April. The lad on the extreme right told his captors that he was 12 years old.

from Carlyle's *History of Friedrich II of Prussia*, telephoned the Fuehrer in a frenzy of excitement as soon as he heard the news, his face eerily lit by the fires of Berlin: 'My Fuehrer, I congratulate you. It is written in the stars that the second half of April will be the turning point for us.' For a few hours there was something approaching exhilaration in the Bunker. Hitler told the valet Misch that soon the Russians and Americans would be exchanging artillery barrages over its concrete canopy. The mood passed. Later Speer recalled, 'Hitler sat exhausted, looking both liberated and dazed, as he slumped in his chair. But I sensed that he was still without hope.'

On Sunday 15 April Hitler's mistress Eva Braun arrived in the Bunker. Since the middle of March she had been living in her private apartments in the Chancellery. One of the SS guard mordantly observed, 'The angel of death has arrived'. At the same time US 9th Army's commander, General Simpson, was summoned to 12th Army Group's headquarters at Wiesbaden. There he was told that he was to halt on the Elbe. He returned to break the news to Brigadier-General Hinds, whose US 2nd Armoured Division was already on the river's eastern bank: 'We're not going to Berlin, Sid. This is the end of the war for us.'

At 5 am on the following morning three red flares soared into the sky above the Küstrin bridgehead. Moments later 20,000 artillery pieces erupted in a furious bombardment, engulfing the German front line, setting forests ablaze and, in a weird atmospheric distortion, sending a hot, debris-laden wind howling back towards Berlin. Then the battlefield was illuminated by a phalanx of 143 searchlights, their

A captured German officer is interrogated in a Red Army command post.

Snow still clings to the verges and civilian vehicles clog the roads as men of General Heinrici's Army Group Vistula wait for an onslaught from General Rokossovsky's 2nd Belorussian Front.

A German 88 in familiar anti-tank role on the Eastern Front, March 1945.

The forgotten front and the end of a nine-month slog. A bridge across the Po in northern Italy, 28 April. US 10th Mountain Division were the first to reach the Po, on 22 April.

beams slicing through the dense smoke and dust-clouds raised by the bombardment. Zhukov's offensive had begun. To the south Konev advanced in equally spectacular fashion, laying down a 250-mile smoke screen to cover his crossing of the Neisse. On Zhukov's front thousands of Red Army soldiers scorned to wait for assault boats or the completion of pontoon bridges, flinging themselves into the Oder. To a watching Russian officer they seemed like 'a huge army of ants, floating across the water on leaves and twigs. The Oder was swarming with boatloads of men, rafts full of supplies, log floats supporting guns. Everywhere were the bobbing heads of men as they swam or floated across.'

For two days Zhukov was held up in a bitter fight for the Seelow heights, a horseshoe-shaped bluff four miles west of the Küstrin bridgehead. By the evening of the 19th the Oder line had been prised open on a 44-mile front, and on the following day – Hitler's 56th birthday – Red Army troops breached the outer north-west defence perimeter of Berlin. Shortly before 2pm the long-range guns of 79th Rifle Corps (3rd Shock Army) opened fire directly on the city. Their shells plummeted into the fires started by the last great Allied bombing raid of the European war.

The Fuehrer's birthday was marked by a special stamp issue and a rather more practical extra allocation of food rations to Berlin's civilian population: one pound of bacon or sausage, one half pound of rice or oatmeal, one half pound of dried lentils, peas or beans, one can of vegetables, two pounds of sugar, about one ounce of coffee, a small package of a coffee substitute and some fats. They were to last eight days and were given the sinister nickname *Himmelsfahrtrationen*, 'Ascension Day Rations'.

As the end drew near in Germany, civil order collapsed. Here German civilians loot an abandoned train. The journalist Margaret Bourke-White recorded a similar scene near Frankfurt, where a train full of clothing was broken open: 'A German *Hausfrau* came running down the railroad tracks towards us. Her arms were so full of silk pants and underclothes that she was scattering a pink trail behind her, laughing and crying at the same time, "Germany is kaput! Might as well loot".'

BALTIC SEA

Rugen

Stralsund

Peenemünde

Treptow

Rostock

Swinemünde

Anklam

BRIT.
2nd
ARMY

Wismar

Gustrow

Neubrandenburg

Stettin

Stargrad

2nd
BELORUSSIAN
FRONT
(Rokossovsky)

Schwerin

Neustrelitz

Ludwigslust

ARMY GROUP
VISTULA
(Heinrici)

Dömitz

Pritzwalk

Templin

Schwedt

Randow

Oder

Elbe

Wittenberge

Neuruppin

Zehdenick

Finow Canal

1st BELORUSSIAN
FRONT (Zhukov)

STEINER

Honenzollern
Canal

Eberswalde

Wriezen

Oranienburg

US 9th ARMY

Kustrin

Stendal

Havel

BERLIN

Muncheberg

Seelow

Tangemünde

Eurstenwalde

Brandenburg

Potsdam

Frankfurt

Eisenhuttenstadt

Magdeburg

Zossen

Oder

Luckenwalde

Juterbog

Guben

Spree

1st
UKRAINIAN
FRONT
(Konev)

Bernburg

Salle

Dessau

Cottbus

Forst

Triebel

APRIL 25/MAY 3
OCCUPIED BY US
& BRITISH FORCES

Schlieben

Spremberg

US 1st
ARMY

Mulde

Torgau

Schwartzheide

Halle

APRIL 25 US & RUSSIAN
FORCES MEET

Merseburg

Leipzig

Riesa

Grossenhain

Kamenz

Görlitz

Colditz

Bautzen

ARMY GROUP
CENTRE
(Schörner)

Dresden

Pirna

Neisse

Sudeten Mts.

| | Front line April 16, 1945 |
| Russian attacks April 16/18 |
| Front line April 18 |
| Russian attacks April 19/May 8 |
| Front line May 8 |
| German counter attacks |
| Surrounded German pockets |
| Berlin defence line |

0   50 Miles

0   80 Kilometres

CZECHOSLOVAKIA

The encirclement of Berlin and the Allies' meeting on the Elbe.

That afternoon there was a birthday reception in the Bunker at which the Nazi paladins – Speer, Bormann, Goebbels, Goering, Ribbentrop – gathered for the last time. Then Hitler left the Bunker for his final public appearance. Bent and trembling, he inspected a line of troops drawn up for him in the Chancellery garden – men of SS Frundsberg Division, a detachment from the beleaguered Army Group Courland and a platoon of Hitler Jugend. The film camera caught the Fuehrer tweaking the cheeks of one of the boy defenders of Berlin. Later that day, at the military conference, Hitler resisted the advice that he leave Berlin for the south, agreeing only to the establishment of a northern and southern command in case Germany was split in two by the Allied advance. Then Hitler's confederates took their leave. Glistening with sweat, Goering announced that he had 'extremely urgent tasks in south Germany', but Hitler merely stared vacantly beyond him. The exodus had begun. In the suburb of Charlottenburg a housewife watched a naval officer 'with lots of gold braid on his uniform' drive off in a large staff car crammed with luggage. A neighbour told her, 'The rats are leaving the sinking ship. That was Admiral Raeder.'

On the 21st, on Konev's front, tank troops of Rybalko's 6th Tank Corps overran the German High Command's abandoned headquarters at Zossen. In the massive underground shelters telephones still rang and teleprinters spewed out frantic messages

Hitler's last public appearance, in the Chancellery garden on his 56th birthday, 20 April.

from disintegrating fronts. On the consoles the departing Germans had placed hastily written notices in schoolboy Russian, 'Do not damage these installations'.

From the Bunker came a ceaseless stream of orders – irrational, contradictory, none of them capable of fulfilment. General von Manteuffel, whose 3rd Panzer Army was all that was left of Army Group Vistula, observed, 'I have no doubt that on Hitler's maps there is a little flag saying 7th Panzer Division, even though it got here without a single tank, truck, piece of artillery or even a machine-gun. We have an army of ghosts.' On the 21st General Koller, the Luftwaffe Chief of Staff, spent most of the day in a gruelling telephone marathon with the Fuehrer: 'In the evening between 8.30 and nine he is again on the telephone. "The Reich Marshal (Goering) is maintaining a private army in Karinhall. Dissolve it at once and … place it under SS Obergruppenfuehrer Steiner", and he hangs up. I am still considering what this is supposed to mean when Hitler calls again: "Every available Air Force man in the area between Berlin and the coast as far as Stettin and Hamburg is to be thrown into the attack I have ordered in the north-east of Berlin", and there is no answer to my question of where the attack is supposed to take place; he has already hung up.'

GIs shake hands with liberated British and Commonwealth POWs.

The attack which so puzzled Koller never took place. 'Army Group Steiner', another of the flags on Hitler's map, had been ordered to sweep down from Eberwalde, north of Berlin, on to Zhukov's right flank. But Army Group Steiner did not exist. In the confusion which followed Hitler's orders, the Russians broke through Berlin's outer defensive ring and pushed into the city.

'FORTRESS BERLIN'

'Fortress Berlin' was the last of Hitler's illusions. In mid-April the fortifications expert, General Max Pemsel, had taken one look at the city's defences and declared them to be 'utterly futile, ridiculous'. It was not until March that any serious consideration had been given to the defence of Berlin, and by then it was far too late. Under the direction of the city commandant, General Reymann, a makeshift 'obstacle belt' had been thrown up in a broken ring 30 miles outside the capital. On the hastily prepared defence maps, slit trenches and isolated pill boxes were marked as major strongpoints. The second ring was improvised around Berlin's railway system, whose cuttings, culverts, sidings and overhead railways would have provided excellent man-made obstacles and a formidable barrier to tanks, had there been enough troops to man them. The last-ditch defence ring – codenamed *Zitadelle* – lay at the heart of the city and contained nearly all the government buildings. Radiating from its inner ring were eight wedge-shaped command sectors, labelled clockwise from A to H. Within the command sectors were six huge flak towers, massive concrete ziggurats impervious to bombs and artillery.

Reymann estimated that 200,000 fully-trained and equipped troops would be needed to defend Berlin's 321 square miles. At his disposal were 60,000 *Volkssturm* and a motley collection of Hitler Jugend, engineers, policemen, and anti-aircraft crew. Reymann recalled, 'Their weapons came from every country that Germany had fought with or against. Besides our own issues there were Italian, Russian, French, Czech, Belgian, Dutch, Norwegian and English guns.' Although a big cache of Greek bullets was remachined to fit the Italian rifles, few of the *Volkssturm* were issued with more than five rounds per rifle.

The sight of the flimsy barricades and improvised tank traps thrown up in Berlin's streets prompted the grim joke that it would take the Red Army at least two hours and fifteen minutes to break through them – two hours laughing their heads off and fifteen minutes smashing them down. But it was impossible to laugh off the atrocity stories that were spread through the city by the columns of refugees straggling in from the east. They added a macabre finishing touch to years of Nazi propaganda. Goebbels' assistant Dr Werner Naumann observed, 'our propaganda as to what the Russians are like, as to what the population can expect from them in Berlin, has been so successful that we have reduced the Berliners to a state of sheer terror.' Many Berliners decided to commit suicide rather than fall into the hands of the Red Army. A quick-acting cyanide-based 'KCB' pill was much in demand.

THE WAR IS LOST

On the 22nd the crisis point was reached in the Bunker. Berlin was now cut off on three sides, and Soviet tanks had been reported to the west of the city. At the midday briefing Hitler lost his self-control, turning blue in the face and raging against the cowardice, incompetence and treachery of the assembled military. Finally he blurted out that the war was lost – the unmentionable had at last been

Soviet tanks roll into Berlin. The Russians advanced not only through the streets but also through the courtyards, basements and buildings. In this fashion they captured entire blocks of the city. In one day troops of Zhukov's 1st Belorussian Front captured 600 city blocks.

admitted. Keitel and Jodl were free to leave and conduct operations as best they could. Hitler declared that he would never leave Berlin. As he was in no physical condition to fight, and could never contemplate capture and exhibition in a 'Moscow zoo', he would commit suicide. Any negotiating that remained to be done was to be left to Goering.

Slowly Hitler got a grip on himself. In his deep, mellifluous baritone Goebbels calmed him and agreed to remain in the Bunker with his family. When, on the following day, two of Hitler's secretaries pleaded to stay with him, he displayed his sentimental streak with a moist-eyed sigh, 'Ah, if only my generals were as brave as my women.' Then he rose to kiss Eva Braun on the lips, something he had never been seen to do before in public. With the help of the drugs administered by his valet he had achieved a kind of serenity. Later that day he received Speer, who had flown in from Hamburg to bid farewell to his patron. When Speer confessed that for weeks he had been striving to thwart Hitler's scorched-earth orders, the Fuehrer showed no emotion.

GÖTTERDÄMMERUNG

On 25 April Zhukov's and Konev's fronts met to the west of Berlin. On the same day elements of Bradley's 12th Army Group and Konev's 1st Ukrainian Front made contact at Torgau on the Elbe, a brief demonstration of comradeship in arms. In the Bunker hopes now rested on General Wenck's 12th Army, to the west of Berlin. In the

Link-up on the Elbe. Soviet military policewomen mount guard with an American sentry at Torgau. The efficient-looking woman on the left is Karuma Galemua, from Astrakhan, who fought at Stalingrad and had 42 dead Germans to her credit.

The Red Flag flies over the Reichstag.

early hours of 23 April Keitel arrived at Wenck's headquarters and with much pointed waving of his field marshal's baton ordered him to turn east and drive through Potsdam to Berlin. 'The battle for Berlin has begun', Keitel declared portentously. In truth it was already over, as Wenck well knew. He heard Keitel out, but had already made his own plans. 12th Army was to 'play it by the book', shifting towards Berlin but not abandoning its position on the Elbe. In this way a corridor could be kept open to the west. Wenck's army was already surrounded by over half a million refugees and appeals by Keitel to save the life of Hitler no longer had any meaning. In the Bunker the unanswered cry *'Wo ist Wenck?'* was to echo round the walls of Hitler's cubby-hole as the Third Reich slid into oblivion.

In Berlin the situation was desperate. Water and public transport systems had finally broken down. Food warehouses in the suburbs had been overrun by the Russians and in the city stocks were down to two or three days. On 22 April the telegraph office closed down after receiving its last message, from Tokyo, 'Good Luck to You All'. Looting broke out. The huge Karstadt store department store in the Hermannplatz was ransacked by a mob before it was dynamited by the SS, who were determined to deny the Russians the vast quantities of supplies salted away in its basement. Flying SS court martial

squads roamed the shattered city, shooting or stringing up from the lamp posts those they deemed to be 'deserters'.

Now the eight Soviet armies which had encircled Berlin drove into the centre of the city in a series of relentless concentric attacks. The S-Bahn ring was breached on the 26th and by nightfall on the 27th 'Fortress Berlin' had been squeezed down to an east-west belt ten miles long and three miles wide. The streets were strewn with the dead – *Volkssturm*, Red Army soldiers, women who had crept up from their cellars to fill a pail of water from a standpipe and had been

Two impressions
by the artist Anthony Gross of
the link-up on the Elbe.

German troops flood over a
pontoon bridge to surrender to
the British 2nd Army.

WARNING!
KEEP CORRECT
SPACING, OR
BRIDGE WILL
SINK !

blown to smithereens by Russian shells. Nor was there safety in the
cellars, for the Russians outflanked the street defences of the
Zitadelle by smashing their way through courtyards, buildings and
basements, blasting their way through party walls and leaving a trail
of rape and destruction behind them. A stunned populace submitted
with bewilderment to that characteristically Russian mixture of
savagery and sudden, unexpected generosity. A Red Army man might
rape a woman and then reappear, bearing presents of food, to protect
her against others. Dazed Hitler Jugend were disarmed, given a cuff

round the ear and packed off home. Near Potsdam, Red Army infantrymen looted the UFA film studios, dancing crazily in the streets in a weird assortment of costumes while the bullets still whistled around their heads.

On the night of the 26th the first Russian shells struck the Chancellery, sending vibrations through the Bunker as tons of masonry toppled into the street below. The defences inside the *Zitadelle* buckled and threatened to give way. By 28 April, Panzer Division 'Munchberger' had been forced back from its front on the Tempelhof Airfield, just inside the S-Bahn ring, to improvised positions round the Anhalter Station, less than half a mile away from

Time runs out as desperate attempts are made to cross the Elbe to the safety of the Western Allies' lines on 7 May. At 2.41 that morning General Jodl had signed the instrument of unconditional surrender at Eisenhower's HQ in Rheims.

the Chancellery. Here they joined the 'Nordland' Division under the command of SS General Gustav Krukenberg. Krukenberg's 'division' was at little more than battalion strength. As a sector commander in the centre of Berlin, his command post was a subway car without either light or telephones.

Around Krukenberg's subway car swarmed hundreds of refugees seeking the safety of the underground platforms. Overhead was the dull, regular thump of impacting Soviet artillery shells. Every so often a close hit would send chunks of masonry spinning into the crowds huddled on the platforms. A surreal touch was added by the occasional arrival of a train, rolling slowly on to an unknown destination.

Men of US 9th Army greet troops of General Konev's 1st Ukrainian Front at Appollensdorf on 30 April.

Then water began to flow through the tunnels. In a bid to prevent the Russians from advancing through them, engineers had been ordered to blow the bulkheads which separated the tunnels from the Landwehr Canal. There was a mad scramble to get above ground – a scene graphically reconstructed after the war in G.W. Pabst's film, *Der Letzte Akt*. Thousands were reported to have died in the tunnels that day, but it is likely that casualties were far fewer. After the initial flood the waters subsided and then the tunnels filled up gradually. The official who was in charge of pumping out the subways in the autumn of 1945 stated that the majority of the bodies found there were of people who had died of their wounds before being placed there.

That night, with the Red Army less than a mile away, Hitler was dealt the final blow. At about 10pm an officer of the Propaganda Ministry handed him a copy of a Reuter's report that Reichsfuehrer-SS Heinrich Himmler had contacted the Swedish diplomat Count Bernadotte in order to negotiate a surrender in the West. Hitler flew into a terrible rage. Goering's treachery could be dismissed as the aberration of a preposterous drug addict. But the defection of 'der treue Heinrich' – the one subordinate on whose loyalty Hitler could depend absolutely – was the bitterest stroke of all. It had been a week since Hitler had admitted to his commanders that the war was lost

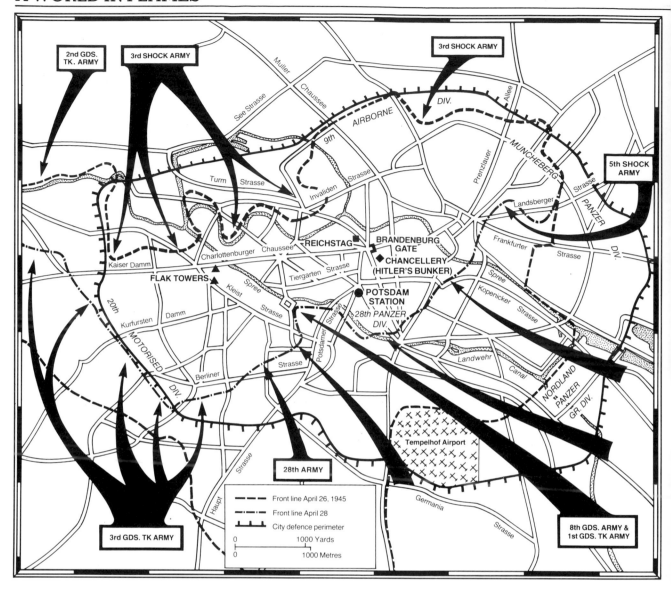

The Red Army's thrusts into Berlin.

and that he intended to commit suicide. Now, after a characteristic period of hesitation and wavering, he made up his mind. Events followed in swift succession. SS General Hermann Fegelein, Himmler's liaison officer and Eva Braun's brother-in-law, was brought to the Bunker, interrogated, then taken away and shot. The new commander-in-chief of the Luftwaffe, Field Marshal Ritter von Greim, who had been stranded – badly wounded – in the Bunker since the evening of the 24th, was ordered to fly out of Berlin with the test pilot Hanna Reitsch to arrest Himmler. They took off from Berlin's East-West axis in a small Arado, shells bursting around them, a sea of fire raging below. After their departure, in the small hours of 29 April Hitler married Eva Braun. The ceremony, conducted by a minor official in the Propaganda Ministry, Walter Wagner, was a model of petit-bourgeois respectability. Hitler and Eva Braun affirmed that they were of pure Aryan descent and were free of hereditary diseases, and were declared man and wife. In her excitement Eva Braun began to sign her maiden name on the wedding certificate, then crossed out the letter B and wrote 'Eva Hitler, née Braun'. With prim bureaucratic efficiency Wagner changed the date on the certificate from 28 to 29 April. Within an hour Wagner, now back on duty with the *Volkssturm*, was fatally shot through the head.

After the wedding there was a melancholy little reception in Hitler's suite. Amid the clink of champagne glasses the conversation ranged for the last time over the glories of times past. At about 2am Hitler retired with a secretary to dictate his political testament. Like the Bourbons, he had learnt nothing and forgotten nothing. The testament concluded, 'Above all I charge the leaders of the nation and those under them to scrupulous observance of the laws of race and to merciless opposition to the universal poisoner of all peoples, international Jewry.'

Goering and Himmler were expelled from the Party and deprived of their now meaningless offices of state. Admiral Doenitz was named as Hitler's successor in the posts of President, Minister of War and Supreme Commander of the Armed Forces. Goebbels and Bormann – whose insinuating influence runs through the testament – received their own empty rewards, the Chancellorship and the post of Party Minister.

Three men were selected to deliver copies of the testament to Doenitz's headquarters at Ploen in Schleswig Holstein and to the last commander-in-chief of the German Army, Field Marshal Schoerner, now in Munich. An additional message was despatched to Field Marshal Keitel, a stinging dismissal of the General Staff from their Supreme Commander: 'The people and the Wehrmacht have given their all in this long and hard struggle. The sacrifice has been enormous. But my trust has been misused by many people. Disloyalty and betrayal have undermined resistance throughout the war. It was therefore not granted to me to lead the people to victory. The Army General Staff cannot be compared with the General Staff of the First World War. Its achievements were far behind those of the fighting front.'

In the course of the 29th news came of the death of Mussolini and his mistress Clara Petacci – summarily executed by partisans near Lake Como and then suspended by their heels from the roof of a Milan garage to be mutilated and spat on by a jeering crowd. On the same day German forces in Italy capitulated at Caserta. Hitler set about preparing his own end. The effects of the poison capsule he intended to crush between his teeth were tested on his Alsatian bitch Blondi. On the morning of the 30th there was one more military conference. Hitler listened expressionlessly as General Weidling informed him that there was heavy fighting in the Tiergarten and the Potsdamer Platz, only a few blocks away from the Chancellery. Then he lunched with his two secretaries and his vegetarian cook, Fräulein Manzialy. While they toyed with spaghetti and tossed salad, Hitler maundered on about the proper breeding of dogs and ventured the observation – both sinister and ridiculous – that French lipstick was made from grease collected in the Paris sewers. There remained only the last farewell to Goebbels, Bormann and the others who were still in the Bunker, among them the fawning General Krebs, who a month earlier had replaced Guderian as Army Chief of Staff.

At about 3.20pm Hitler and Eva Braun withdrew into the Fuehrer's suite. Outside the door the inhabitants of the Bunker waited. Hitler shot himself with his Walther 7.65 calibre pistol, which he had been carrying in his jacket for several weeks, in all probability simultaneously biting into the poison capsule. Eva Braun took poison. It was an end both melodramatic and tawdry, bearing the imprint of the turn of the century world which had been Hitler's spiritual home. As Joachim Fest observed, Hitler 'lay dead on the bunker sofa like a ruined gambler of the opera-hat era beside his newly-wed mistress. It

Coupons last longer with BEAR BRAND UTILITY STOCKINGS

Daily Mail

LATE WAR NEWS

Sleeping badly? Take two tablets of GENASPRIN at bedtime

NO. 15,285   ONE PENNY   * *   FOR KING AND EMPIRE   WEDNESDAY, MAY 2, 1945

HITLER DEAD, GERMAN RADIO TELLS WORLD

Admiral Doenitz is new Führer: 'The battle goes on'

ADOLF HITLER is dead. Grand Admiral Doenitz, Commander-in-Chief of the German Navy, has been appointed his successor. The German radio gave this news to the world at 10.25 last night in the following words: "It is reported from the Führer's headquarters that our Führer, Adolf Hitler, has fallen this afternoon in his command post in the Reich Chancellery fighting to his last breath against Bolshevism."

"On April 30 [Monday] the Führer appointed Grand Admiral Doenitz as his successor. The Grand Admiral will now speak to the German people."

Admiral Doenitz, who immediately came on the air, said: "My task is to save the German people from annihilation at the hands of Bolshevism. We shall have to fight on against the British and Americans so far as they hinder our aim."

The naming of the admiral as the new Führer comes as a complete surprise.

It suggests that what remains of Germany has been split into two camps—those who wish to fight on, led by Doenitz, and those who want to surrender, led by Himmler.

It is significant that no reference was made in the announcement to Himmler, who has already offered unconditional surrender to Britain and the United States, and is expected to comply with the Allied demand that capitulation must be made also to Russia.

Doenitz said: "German men and women, soldiers of the German Army, our Führer, Adolf Hitler, has fallen. The German people are bowed in sorrow and reverence.

"Our Führer had recognised very early the grim danger of Bolshevism and consecrated his life to the struggle against it.

Nazi radio kept world in suspense

Wagner build-up

By Daily Mail Reporter

BEFORE the announcement of Hitler's death, Hamburg radio held the world in suspense for more than an hour.

From 9 p.m. until 9.30 Wagner's Tannhäuser Overture and a piano concerto by Weber were played.

This was interrupted with the warning "Please stand by for an important announcement" It will be broadcast on this wavelength.

The station went silent for a while.

At 9.40 the stand-by warning was repeated and Wagner's "Twilight of the Gods" was played.

At 9.43 the announcer shouted: "Achtung! Achtung!" the German Broadcasting System is going to give an important German Government announcement for the German people.

The old phrase

V DAY

The full official plans

By Daily Mail Political Correspondent

NEWS that the war in Europe is over will be given by the Prime Minister in a special B.B.C. broadcast This may be given by Mr. Churchill at any hour of the day or night in the very near future.

It will be followed by a broadcast by the King to the Empire, which has been fixed for nine o'clock on the night of VE-Day.

The day following, as well as VE-Day, will be a Public Holiday.

The Home Office letter sent out to local authorities last night suggested the opening of churches and chapels for private prayer on VE-Day, and the ringing of church bells throughout the country.

☆

THE appointment of the Sunday following VE-Day as a Day of Prayer and Thanksgiving to be accompanied by local victory parades in which all representatives of the armed and civil forces in the district shall take part.

The King will attend St. Paul's, in London, on this day and will be represented at special services at Edinburgh, Belfast, and Cardiff.

Local authorities are urged to use such floodlighting facilities as they have, but street lighting will not be restored in full and the dim-out

NO NEWS FROM HIMMLER, BUT

Surrender begins on three fronts

REPORTS received in London late last night indicated that, while no fresh offer of capitulation has been received from Himmler, large German forces on widely separated fronts have begun to surrender piecemeal to the Allies with or without his authority.

Here is the latest position:

DENMARK.—German occupation forces were reported from Stockholm to be evacuating the country with all speed.

NORWAY.—Negotiations are said to be going on for the German garrisons to lay down their arms at the Swedish frontier.

CZECHO-SLOVAKIA: A delegation of German and Czech industrialists was reported by Luxemburg radio to have left Prague to meet Allied representatives and hand over the territories of Bohemia and Moravia.

ITALY: Marshal Graziani and Lieut.-General Pemsel, German Chief of Staff of the Italian Fascist Ligurian Army, last night announced the surrender of that army and ordered all troops to lay down their arms.

Count Bernadotte, on arriving back in Stockholm yesterday, told a Press conference that he had not seen Himmler during his second visit to Denmark and had brought no fresh message from any German authority.

German army scurries out of Denmark

From Daily Mail Correspondent

Busmen to strike to-day

LONDON busmen at Camberwell, Clapham, and Streatham garages decided late last night to go on strike to-day in protest against the summer schedules. Their decision followed an agreement

FOOD SHIPS FOR DUTCH

SHAEF announces Allied and German representatives made agreements for food supply to Dutch by air, sea, and road. Ten air-dropping zones agreed; food ships to enter Rotterdam; and Germans to make available one main road. Supply starts to-day.

---

was a finale in which he dropped out of the period and once again revealed the antique basis of his nature.'

The bodies were carried into the Chancellery garden, laid in a shallow trench, soaked in petrol and then set alight. A few hours later they were buried in a deeper trench dug out of a shell crater. On 3 May they were unearthed by an alert Red Army private, though the credit for the discovery was taken by an NKVD interrogator, Lieutenant-Colonel Ivan Klimenko, who on 5 May exhumed the charred remains from the slime and rubble outside the Bunker.

SURRENDER

Shortly after midnight Goebbels despatched General Krebs to the Russian lines in an attempt to negotiate a partial surrender. In the days of the Nazi-Soviet pact the Russian-speaking Krebs had been publicly embraced by Stalin. Now the grip of the Russian bear was less friendly. Accompanied by an interpreter and an aide, he was escorted to the headquarters of General Chuikov, the defender of Stalingrad. Chuikov had been enjoying a supper with members of his political staff, two war correspondents and the composer Blanter, who had been sent to Berlin to write a victory anthem. When Krebs arrived they were airily passed off by Chuikov as members of his war council, with the exception of Blanter, who was dressed in civilian clothes. He was hastily bundled into a cupboard, where he remained for most of the ensuing conference before passing out through lack of air and crashing into the room at the feet of the astonished Krebs.

Krebs opened the proceedings by telling Chuikov that Hitler was dead. The Russian general played this startling delivery with a straight bat, replying, 'We know that'. Krebs was amazed and insisted on explaining in detail the events of the last few hours. It was the first time that the Russians learned of the existence of the Bunker or, for that matter, of Eva Braun. The talks dragged on for hours, but the Russians had only one answer to Krebs' rambling arguments – unconditional general surrender. Krebs returned empty-handed and a renewed and ferocious Russian barrage descended on the Reichstag and the Chancellery. It was only at this point that Bormann informed Doenitz of the Fuehrer's death. In the Bunker Magda Goebbels poisoned her six children and then committed suicide with her husband in the Chancellery garden. A perfunctory effort was made to burn their bodies; their corpses remained grotesquely charred but recognizable. Curiously, the Russians claimed to have found their bodies back inside the Bunker when it was overrun at midday on 2 May.

The victors: Zhukov and staff officers on the steps of the Reichstag.

The wreckage inside the Chancellery building.

On the night of 1/2 May the surviving inhabitants of the complex bunkers under the Chancellery attempted a mass break-out. Many of them succeeded in making their way out of Berlin, but not Martin Bormann (see Part Three). Early in the morning of 2 May General Weidling surrendered Berlin to the Red Army. At three in the afternoon the Russian guns fell silent.

UNCONDITIONAL SURRENDER

On the evening of 1 May the new German head of state, Admiral Doenitz, broadcast a stark message to the German people: 'My first task is to save Germany from destruction by the advancing Bolshevik enemy. It is to serve this purpose that the struggle continues.' In Doenitz's possession was a captured copy of the Allies' 'Eclipse' plan for the postwar dismemberment of Germany. On 1 May German forces still controlled territory on both sides of the map's east-west demarcation line, holding out the hope that the eastern armies and a huge number of refugees might yet make their way to the zones controlled by the British and the Americans.

Doenitz set about trying to surrender in the West while holding off the Russians in the East. Eisenhower would have none of this, although there was a partial surrender in northern Germany, where Army Group Vistula's line of retreat into Schleswig Holstein had been severed by Montgomery's advance to Lübeck.

Two symbolic views of the end
of the war. In a French poster
the swastika is torn asunder by
the arms of the Allies. A Polish
poster links the collapse of the
Third Reich with a famous
defeat of the Teutonic knights in
the Middle Ages.

A WORLD IN FLAMES

At 5pm on 4 May Admiral Friedeburg and his delegation arrived at Montgomery's headquarters on Lüneburg Heath to surrender all German forces in Holland, north-west Germany and Denmark. Photographs of the event show the grim-faced German officers looking faintly ludicrous as they creak their way across the windy heath in their long leather overcoats, escorted by British counterparts who seem like bank managers in uniform. For the signing, Montgomery was at his most brisk and schoolmasterly. As he recalled, the business was conducted on a 'trestle table covered with an army blanket, an inkpot, an ordinary army pen that you could buy in a shop for twopence ... The Germans were clearly nervous and one of them took out a cigarette ... I looked at him and he put the cigarette away.'

From Lüneburg Admiral Friedeburg went to Eisenhower's headquarters at Rheims, where on 6 May he was joined by General Jodl. Taken to Friedeburg's room, Jodl greeted the Admiral with a cryptic 'Aha'. A few minutes later Friedeburg emerged to ask for coffee and a map of Europe. The Germans were obviously playing for time and Eisenhower issued a brisk ultimatum. Whether or not the Germans delayed, he would close his lines within 48 hours of midnight on 6 May, 'so that no more Germans can get through'. At 2.41am on the morning of 7 May General Jodl signed the instrument of unconditional surrender in Eisenhower's war room which, appropriately, was dominated by a giant mock thermometer mounted on a background of swastikas and bearing a running total of German prisoners in Allied hands. An hour later Eisenhower brought matters to a conclusion with a brief but expressively worded cable to the British and American Chiefs of Staff: 'The mission of the Allied force was fulfilled at 0241, local time, May 7, 1945.'

right Admiral Friedeburg and his aides wait to see Montgomery on Lüneburg Heath.

below right The surrender ceremony at Lüneburg, 6.30pm, 4 May.

The vanquished: bodies and gutted vehicles litter the streets of Berlin after the German surrender.

Part Two

WHEN THE LIGHTS GO ON AGAIN

WHY ARE WE WAITING?

'What strikes me is that the war's ending in just the same phoney way as it began: "It's peace", "It isn't peace", "They've surrendered", "They haven't surrendered". It does bring back those first months when there was and there wasn't a war.'

I n September 1939 the British had drifted into the Phoney War. At the end of April 1945 it seemed as if they were drifting into a Phoney Peace. Armistice Day on 11 November 1918 had come as a sudden, wild explosion of relief. The approach of VE Day was an agonizingly slow process. When it finally arrived it found the British in a characteristic mood of muddle and mild exasperation with authority.

For the British the Second World War was an unconscionable time ending. Churchill recognized the crucial moment – 11 December 1941 – when Hitler declared war on the United States: 'So we have won after all.' The war still had three and a half years to run, but within a year the British were already turning their thoughts towards peace.

On 1 December 1942 – three weeks after Montgomery's victory at El Alamein – the Beveridge Report was published, providing a blueprint for Britain's postwar welfare state. As Beveridge wrote in the report, if the Allies could 'plan for a better peace even while waging war, they will win together two victories which in truth are indivisible.' Significantly, *Went the Day Well?*, an Ealing film released in October 1943, was framed between a prologue and epilogue set in a time *after* the war has ended. The end of the war also appeared on the horizon in Frank Launder and Sidney Gilliat's *Millions Like Us*, a populist drama set in a war factory which was released at the same time as *Went the Day Well?* Brusque north country works foreman Eric Portman rehearses his misgivings about romance with upper-class 'mobile woman' Anne Crawford with these words: 'The world's roughly made up of two types of people – you're one sort and I'm another. Oh, we're together now there's a war on – we need to be. What's going to happen when it's over? Shall we go on like this or shall we slide back ... I'm not marrying you, Jennifer, till I'm sure.'

Throughout 1944 small signs of peace began to nibble away at the panoply of wartime restrictions. In February the Board of Trade relaxed the regulation which, with the aim of saving textiles, prohibited turn-ups on men's trousers, limited the number of pockets on their jackets and snipped two inches off their shirt tails. Hugh Dalton, President of the Board of Trade, explained the removal of the restriction with the memorable comment, 'On the whole we have done something to lift the morale of the country – particularly the morale of the men. The morale of the women has always been high, but that of the men has been depressed by not having enough pockets.'

In September 1944 Civil Defence outside the London area was virtually disbanded, and on the 17th of that month the 'blackout' was

Above all, perhaps, 8 May was Churchill's day, although his star was soon to wane.

replaced by the 'dimout', although it still remained in force in all coastal areas and for a distance of five miles inland. By no means did everyone rush to remove the blackout material from the curtains, and when they did there were often some unpleasant surprises. A civil servant from the village of Branscombe in Devon discovered that removing the blackout was an extremely messy business as the dust and dead insects which had accumulated behind the shutters for five years now descended on him in an avalanche. After the rigours of 'make do and mend', economy took precedence over elation at the disappearance of an unwelcome restriction. A Birmingham woman recalled, 'We did not go mad and burn the materials. They came in handy for years.'

On 2 December the Lord Mayor of London presided over a dinner at the Mansion House to mark the standing down of the Home Guard. The after-dinner speeches were rudely interrupted by a sudden reminder of war when a V-2 exploded with a deafening roar only a few hundred yards away. The V-2 rockets had taken up where the V-1s had left off. On 7 September 1944, Duncan Sandys, chairman of the government's Counter-Measures committee, confidently told a press conference, 'Except possibly for a few last shots the battle of London is over.' Within 24 hours the first V-2 fell on Chiswick, in London, with a tremendous detonation which was heard all over the capital. It was not until 10 November that Churchill admitted in the House of Commons that the Germans were bombarding London with

An American military policeman examines a V-2 rocket in the underground assembly plant at Nordhausen. The town was occupied on 10 April 1945 by troops of US 1st Army who took over the plant and liberated the slave labourers imprisoned in the adjoining concentration camp.

long-range rockets – during the government's long silence they had earned the ironic tag of 'flying gas mains'. In the same month Deptford was the scene of the worst V-2 disaster, when a rocket scored a direct hit on a Woolworth's crowded with Saturday-morning shoppers. One hundred and sixty died, most of them women and children.

The V-2 was preceded by no warning – if you didn't hear it, you bought it. For most fortunate souls outside the blast radius there was a bright flash in the sky followed by a supersonic bang and then an ear-splitting explosion. The V-2 barrage was an unnerving experience and the art historian James Lees-Milne spoke for many Londoners when he described the threat of the rockets as 'a perpetual sword of Damocles over one's head … The V-2 has become far more alarming than the V-1, quite contrary to what I thought at first, because it gives no sound. One finds oneself waiting for it, and jumping out of one's skin at the slightest bang or unexpected noise, like a car backfiring or even a door slam.'

The last of Hitler's 'revenge weapons' fell to earth on 27 March 1945, at Orpington in Kent. In all, 1,050 V-2s were spotted by observers, 518 of which hit London, killing 2,754 people and severely injuring 6,523.

A less dramatic but infinitely more persistent reminder of the privations of war was the grim winter of 1944-45, with its seemingly endless queues and fuel shortages. A December entry in the diary of a London housewife captures the glum mood of the last winter of the war: 'Absolutely nothing of note this week; fog, which made me lose my way coming home … ice and frost … the usual accompaniment of bangs from rockets … sirens one evening early and two doodles droning over the house … a hateful boil on my neck … People in the office have colds, pains and aches in limbs and crawl about with overcoats on and shawls draped about them … With only cardboard and mica windows and no doors or walls to keep out the draughts it is pretty freezing and it seems our legs will never be felt again.' It was in the winter of 1944 that hopes of a speedy victory had been dashed by Hitler's offensive in the Ardennes, but by the following March it was clear that Germany was on the verge of collapse. On 1 March Harold Nicolson, one of the small band of National Labour MPs in the

In the slush of January 1945 Mrs Mary Dyett moves into the first prefabricated home built after Duncan Sandys took over the Ministry of Works. This is one of a group of prefabs erected on a bomb-site in Greenwich, south-east London.

WHEN THE LIGHTS GO ON AGAIN

Commons, wrote in his diary: 'As we [Nicolson and Anthony Eden] were walking to our seats through the tangle of the smoking room we passed the Evening News spread out over the back of an arm chair. It bore the headline "Tanks mass for Cologne". Anthony tapped it as he passed with the back of his fingers. "I think it's almost over, Harold." "What–the offensive?" "No, my dear, the WAR".'

But with the end so near there was already a feeling of anti-climax in the air. A working-class London housewife questioned by a Mass-Observation* interviewer expressed the general mood of frustration: 'Well, I don't know. I'd have felt more excited if it had finished last summer, when we all thought it would. Somehow I don't feel so excited now – I feel sort of deadened – as if when I see the headlines "Germany Capitulates", I shall be just thinking, "So what?" I mean everything will go on as before, and there will be less food than ever, and I don't suppose my husband will come home for months and years, and they will nag us about winning the peace or something, just as they nagged us about winning the war.'

However, a bus conductress questioned during the Easter holiday was more optimistic: 'Wouldn't you think they *know*? What's the good of them going on fighting? They know they're beat. I'd give in if I was them. Did you hear the news this morning? Patton has advanced 55 miles in 24 hours. But I can't help thinking that Montgomery's front is the important one.....It'll all be over in a fortnight. This is the last Bank Holiday I'll have to work.'

FLAGS AND BUNTING

Frustrating as it was, the snail's pace approach of peace enabled people in Britain to adjust themselves to the fact of it and, stimulated by the huge crop of rumours, to experience in advance its pleasures and excitements. The rush to buy flags and bunting in readiness for VE Day began in the first week of April, as Model's Army Group B was encircled in the Ruhr pocket. In London the counters of the West End stores suddenly sprouted small forests of patriotic flags and streamers. Business was brisk, and by common consent Selfridges' flag department was the best stocked and its displays the most imaginative. Large and small Union Jacks took pride of place alongside flags of the colonies and banners bearing portraits of George VI and the legend 'God Save the King'. Another popular item was a 'Welcome Home' flag for returning POWs. The Selfridges buyer confided, 'We've been busy for the last two to three weeks, but we haven't got to the same pitch as we did last September when Paris fell. We did amazing business then – people simply thought the war was going to end by October. But business is warming up... The average person pays 25/- to 30/- for a flag and we do a considerable trade in streamers at 7/3d.'

Everywhere in Britain high street shop windows displayed Victory

From the first week in April shops and traders enjoyed a boom in sales of Victory flags, scarves, hats, favours and badges.

---

* *Mass-Observation was founded in 1937 by a young and radical group which included Humphrey Jennings, Tom Harrisson, Kathleen Raine and William Empson. Their aim was to conduct a massive investigation into all aspects of British social life, and one of their first projects was a study of Bolton and Blackpool, the Worktown Project. In the war the running of Mass-Observation was centralized in London and in 1940-41 the group worked in co-operation with the Ministry of Information. After the formal relationship came to an end Mass-Observation continued to provide several government departments with information for the duration of the war.*

scarves, ribbons and rosettes – even hairslides, which were a shilling apiece at Woolworths. Bourne and Hollingsworth reported a roaring trade in Victory scarves at 24/6d, but as a counter assistant pointed out to one buyer, 'It's ever so pretty, but after the war you can't wear that. You'll want to get away from the war.'

A month later, when peace was just around the corner, flags had become just one more item on the long list of 'shortages' and any attempt to buy one became a gruelling undertaking. On 7 May – VE Day-1 – all Derry and Toms could offer shoppers were gilt cardboard crests in two sizes – large at 5/- and small at 3/-. Nevertheless, wartime habits died hard – in Barkers one dauntless shopper was overheard to say, 'I have been in so many queues since the war began, it'll be a change to be in a flag queue.'

In the windows of the Galeries Lafayette in Regent Street a huge display of flags surrounded the portraits of Stalin, Roosevelt and Churchill. Roosevelt was wearing a black scarf around his throat, lending a melancholy touch after his death on 12 April and prompting one wag to suggest that he was now appropriately in mourning for himself.

THE DEMON KING LEAVES THE STAGE

No mourning accompanied the announcement of Hitler's death. At 9.30 on the evening of 1 May Hamburg Radio had warned the German people that 'a grave and important announcement' was about to be made. Then, to the strains of Bruckner's Seventh Symphony, came the news of Hitler's death. 'It is reported from the Fuehrer's headquarters that our Fuehrer, Adolf Hitler, fighting to the last breath against Bolshevism, fell for Germany this afternoon in his operational command post in the Reich Chancellery...' At 10.20 Admiral Doenitz came on the air to announce Hitler's death and his own succession. Near the Baltic port of Lübeck a British prisoner of war, Lieutenant-Commander John Casson, heard Doenitz's announcement in remarkable circumstances. Casson and hundreds of other POWs had been on a long forced march, under armed guard, away from the Russians and towards the British 2nd Army. While they rested, one of

A German POW greets Hitler's death with a smile as he reads the banner headline in The Stars and Stripes.

the guards asked the German-speaking Casson if he would like to listen to the latest news bulletin from Radio Hamburg. (Casson did not inform him that the POWs had been keeping up with events by listening to the BBC on their own improvised receiver.) After entertaining his hosts with some conjuring tricks while they tuned in, Casson and his captors listened to Doenitz's broadcast to the German nation. There was silence until the words, 'Der Fuehrer ist todt', whereupon one young German soldier swore 'Scheisse', an older one murmured, 'Gott sei dank', and a third merely threw his cap on the floor. Within an hour British troops had liberated Casson and his fellow POWs. Now the captured were the captors and that night Casson sat around a campfire with some of his former guards talking in German about philosophy.

Also among the first to hear these broadcasts were men of 6th Battalion, the Royal Welch Fusiliers, who were advancing on Hamburg. Huddled round their command radio set in a captured farmhouse they listened in to the announcements from Hamburg Radio. The following morning they decided to leave behind a memento of the occasion on the village monument, which commemorated a visit by Hitler in 1935. One of the Fusiliers – a stonemason in civilian life – chipped out the end of the story – 'KAPUT 1945'.

In Britain Hitler's departure from this world was accompanied by a similar element of bathos. Ten minutes after Doenitz had gone off the air there was a news flash on the General Forces Programme, repeating the announcement of Hitler's death and Doenitz's proclamation of his own succession. Then it continued with 'Music While You Work'. Listeners to the Home Service had to wait another ten minutes as the BBC declined to interrupt 'Evening Prayers'.

The demon king had left the stage with a final flourish of lies, leaving a curious emptiness in many people's lives. The report was greeted with a great deal of scepticism – perhaps Hitler was still alive. A Mass-Observation interviewer recorded a typical reaction: 'He's not dead – don't you believe it. They've got him hidden away somewhere to bring him out in ten years when they think we'll have forgotten about it and start the business all over again.' Some people launched themselves into the realm of fantasy: 'I think that he is dead – he died when there was an attempt on his life. But he's got five doubles, you see, so that you can't quite tell.' (This man was nearer to the truth than he realized. On 2 May Lieutenant-Colonel Ivan Klimenko, an NKVD interrogator, discovered the body of a murdered Hitler double in a water tank in the Chancellery garden.) There was a lingering feeling that, somehow, Hitler was invulnerable, a man whom it was impossible to kill. This added yet another element of uncertainty to a situation alive with rumours: 'All the rumours! Hitler's dead, Hitler's dying, Hitler's only having his face lifted. Some people say Churchill will announce peace on the nine o'clock news tonight. Oh, they're saying everything. My ears are dropping off with the rumours I've heard. The one thing you can take for certain is that Mussolini is dead.'

THE ALLIES ENTER CONCENTRATION CAMPS

A far grimmer note was struck by the release of newsreel film of the concentration camps overrun by the Allies. Buchenwald was liberated by US troops on 11 April; Bergen-Belsen, overrun by the British, followed on the 15th. The first British soldier to enter Belsen was a young intelligence officer, Derrick Sington. When he entered the camp's inner compound, 'It reminded me of the entrance to a zoo. We came in to the smell of ordure – like the smell of a monkey house. A sad, blue smoke floated like ground mist between the low buildings. I had tried to imagine the interior of a concentration camp, but I had not imagined it like this. Nor had I imagined the strange simian throng who crowded the barbed wire fences surrounding the compounds, and the obscene striped penitentiary suits.' Two weeks later, on 29 April, US troops arrived at Dachau, situated in the pleasant countryside outside Munich. One of Dachau's prisoners, a Dutch airman, wrote in his diary, '17.28 first American comes through the entrance. Dachau free!!! Indescribable happiness. Insane howling.' Shortly afterwards an American company commander lost control of his men who, unhinged by the terrible spectacle of the liberated camp, machine-gunned to death 120 unarmed SS guards.

In the days leading up to the German surrender the atrocity films

left A woman liberated from Belsen concentration camp, by Eric Taylor.

right GIs and inmates in the compound of a concentration camp shortly after its liberation.

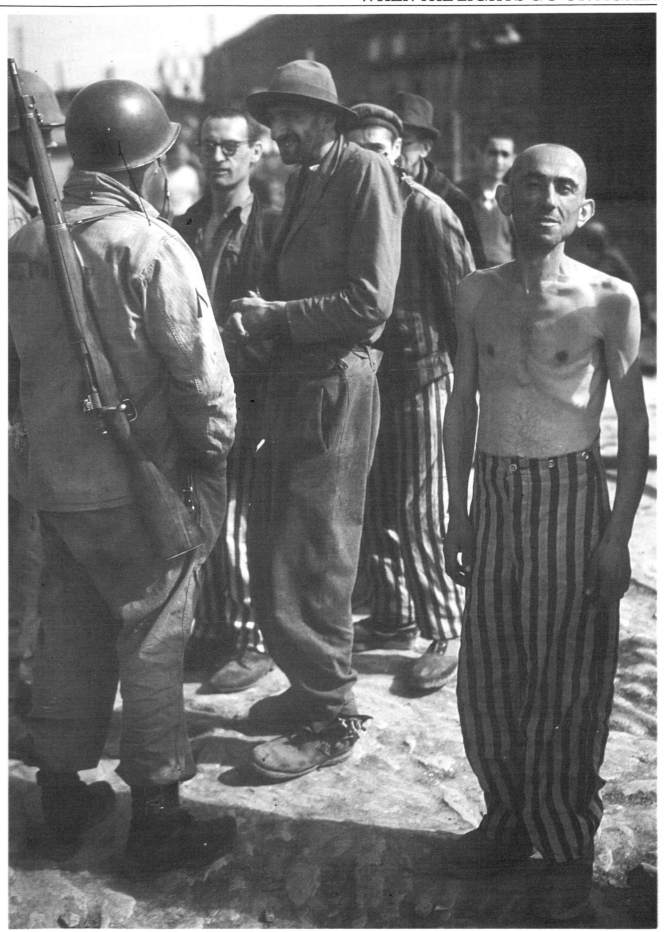

began to appear in British cinemas. A London woman recorded her impressions of a visit to the Newsreel Cinema where a report on the liberation of Belsen was part of the programme. She arrived at the end of a Donald Duck cartoon, which was followed by the news and then the special report on Belsen. Immediately afterwards there was another Donald Duck cartoon. During the atrocity film, 'the audience was intensely still…There were occasional sniffs, as of people restraining tears but blowing their noses, and several sounds of sharp in-breathing, particularly as the skeleton-like bodies of those just still alive were shown. A very large number of the audience got up and went out at the end of the film … They filed down the stairs silently … one woman about 35 was covering her eyes with her hands; several others were dabbing their eyes or using handkerchiefs … several others blew their noses violently.'

VE DAY-1

For at least a week before it became a fact the announcement of peace was expected almost hourly. The rush of events was reflected in the headlines of the Daily Express:

Tuesday 1 May: 'Nazi Radio "Goodbye"'

Wednesday 2 May: 'Hitler is Dead'

Thursday 3 May: 'Army of 100,000 Surrenders'

Friday 4 May: 'British Enter Denmark'

Saturday 5 May: 'Germans Surrender Inside Monty's Tent'

Monday 7 May: 'The Last Hours'

'The Last Hours' was an appropriately vague headline, fashioned to cover the uncertainty which surrounded the closing moments of the war. At 2.41am on 7 May General Jodl had put his signature to the instrument of unconditional surrender at General Eisenhower's HQ at Rheims. Operations were to cease at 23.01 hrs (Central European Time) on 8 May. On the afternoon of 7 May, at 2.30pm, the new German Foreign Minister, Schwerin von Krosigk, broadcast to the German people from Flensburg. He had a harsh message for them. 'No one must be under any illusions about the severity of the terms to be imposed on the German people by our enemies. We must now face our fate squarely and unquestioningly … In our nation justice shall be the supreme law and the guiding principle. We must also recognize law as the basis of all relations between nations … Respect for treaties will be as sacred as the aim of our nation to belong to the European family of nations … Then we may hope that the atmosphere of hatred which today surrounds Germany all over the world will give place to a spirit of reconciliation among the nations … May God bless our difficult task.'

The Allied leaders and their staffs now knew that the war was over. The Germans had been told that they had been beaten. But the British and American peoples were, for the moment, to be kept in the dark. The reason lay in the promise given to the Russians by Churchill and Truman that the news would not be released until the surrender had been formally ratified at Zhukov's headquarters in Berlin. Accordingly the cease-fire orders were sent in cipher. At the same time the war correspondents at Eisenhower's headquarters were denied access to telephones and teleprinters.

THE BIG LEAK

Inevitably, one journalist was more enterprising than his colleagues. Edward Kennedy was a highly respected Associated Press man who had been working in Europe since 1935. In the small hours of the morning of 7 May he left Rheims for Paris, where he wrote a 1,500-word story on the surrender and filed it with SHAEF (Supreme Headquarters Allied Expeditionary Force) for despatch. Not surprisingly SHAEF sat on Kennedy's report, but after Schwerin von Krosigk's broadcast the Associated Press man took the law into his own hands and phoned his story through to his agency's office in London. In the best 'Front Page' tradition he told Associated Press, 'This is Ed Kennedy. Germany has surrendered unconditionally. That's official. Make the dateline Rheims, France, and get it out.' Because Kennedy was speaking from France, the censor in London automatically passed the message.

The advance flash reached New York as Kennedy was filing his story on the telephone, and at 9.36am New York Time (3.36pm in London and Rheims) the news spilled out of teleprinters from coast to coast: GERMANY SURRENDERED UNCONDITIONALLY TO THE WESTERN ALLIES AND RUSSIA 2.41 AM FRENCH TIME TODAY.

By now word of the enterprising Kennedy's activities had reached Eisenhower's HQ. Kay Summersby, the Englishwoman who was Eisenhower's driver and confidante, recalled: 'Around 3pm the final blow fell. Beetle (Lieutenant-General Bedell Smith, Eisenhower's Chief of Staff) roared into the office like a madman. Ed Kennedy of Associated Press had smuggled into America a story of the Rheims surrender ... leaving a pack of angry correspondents in France, a group of very upset gentlemen in the Kremlin, 10 Downing Street and the White House – and a very irate Supreme Commander at Rheims.'

SHAEF moved quickly to kill the story. Within two hours it transmitted to American news agencies a communiqué which was a small masterpiece of bureaucratic obfuscation: 'Supreme Headquarters authorize correspondents at 16.45 Paris time (10.45 Eastern Daylight Time) today to state that SHAEF has made nowhere any official statement for publication to that hour concerning the complete surrender of all German armed forces in Europe and that no story to this effect is authorized.'

The message stopped well short of contradicting Kennedy but it sowed the seeds of doubt, capitalizing on an earlier false alarm of 28 April when a casual remark by a senator in San Francisco had stampeded Associated Press into a premature announcement of the German surrender. One of the journalists in San Francisco on 7 May was Alistair Cooke, who was covering the United Nations conference for the Manchester Guardian. Ed Kennedy's story had broken at 6.30am, setting 'the telephones ringing in delegation bedrooms, radio commentators piling into driverless cabs and the presses of local papers triumphantly stamping out the enormous headlines they had set up weeks ago'. After the arrival of the SHAEF message the mood quickly changed: 'The American itch to "jump the gun" has never been rewarded with such public humiliation ... The delegation heads who had announced press conferences today promptly postponed them and it was not until the radio networks returned to their reassuring daily routine of morning serials and cooking recipes that San Franciscans knew that they were back in the world of reality and that the conference delegations could take up the business of peace where they left it last night.'

WHEN THE LIGHTS GO ON AGAIN
NEW YORK CELEBRATES

New Yorkers were not so concerned about jumping the gun. In the words of the New York Times the news 'swept the city with gale velocity. Men and women, utter strangers, shouted it to one another ... housewives screamed it from the windows. Clerks and typists shrilled it from the skyscrapers. River craft east and west took it up and fed the din with sirens and whistle blasts ... Then the great paper and cloth throwing orgy began. Paper in every possible form and description cascaded from a hundred thousand windows – scrap paper, ledgers, playing cards, torn telephone book fragments, stationery, streamers, tickertape.'

Celebrations on New York's Wall Street on VE-1. In the United States VE Day proper was not a public holiday.

The blizzard of paper was followed by a cascade of textiles tossed from the windows of dress manufacturers and wholesalers. The morning air was alive with snaking parabolas described by bales of remnants floating to earth in a blaze of colour: 'Within the hour, 6th, 7th and 8th Avenue and Broadway were eight to ten inches deep in multicolored fabrics.' The New York Times went on to comment sardonically, 'Thrifty passers-by forgot their delirium long enough to salvage some of the larger remnants.'

By midday the celebrations were on a bigger scale than had been seen in 1918. More than a million New Yorkers came out to dance in the streets. Traffic ground to a halt and in Times Square a packed, heaving mass of people swayed and danced until 5pm, when they were brought down to earth by the stern tones of Mayor La Guardia: 'I want all the people of the City of New York who have thoughtlessly left their jobs to go home ... Maybe there's still some fighting going on. You don't know and I don't know ... Let's be patient for just a few more hours.'

After the spontaneous outbursts of 7 May, VE Day in New York was slow to gather pace. Nevertheless this sailor in Times Square seems temporarily careless of President Truman's stern message, broadcast at 9 am: 'Our victory is but half won. The West is free but the East is still in bondage ... when the last Japanese has surrendered unconditionally, then only will our fighting job be done.'

However, patience was in steadily decreasing supply as Americans tuned in their radios hoping to hear news of victory but finding that Normal Service had been resumed after an abortive flurry of victory items earlier in the day. An announcer at CBS departed from his script to express a heartfelt exasperation: 'It's obviously a fact. But not official. Official is official is official. And there, for all the purposes of absolute definition, goes the day we thought might be called VE Day … If the objective of the supernatural powers had been to snafu* the actual end of the war in Europe, so as to save all the waste of the climactic hysteria, nothing could have worked out better.'

BRITISH NEWS BLACKOUT

In Britain on the morning of the 7th, people went about their business uncertain as to whether the day would end as a holiday. The confusions of the preceding week had encouraged widespread cynicism about the authorities' intentions. On 2 May a London office worker had recorded in her diary, 'People in the office were talking about the V holiday – rather cynically on the whole. Someone

By nightfall on 8 May, New Yorkers were beginning to get their second wind. Broadway was lit up and just before 8.30 pm the Statue of Liberty was illuminated. Specially fitted bulbs gave her torch the 'bluish character of living flame'.

* Snafu – a salty American service expression standing for 'Situation normal, all fouled up'.

suggested that the announcement would probably be made about 11 o'clock on Saturday morning, so that except for leaving about an hour early we shouldn't really get any extra holiday at all.' But the weekend had come and gone and apathy had now been overtaken by a feeling of expectancy. News listening became almost obsessive. It seemed as if 7 May was an exaggerated version of the days which had gone before, as everyone waited for the final announcement. In a sense the announcement itself had now assumed merely the importance of a technical detail – the war was clearly over, already slipping into the past. All that remained to be experienced was the arrival of a dramatic moment marking the transition from official war to official peace.

The government did their level best to ensure that everyone was disappointed. As hope receded of Russian agreement, the day dragged by without an announcement. Churchill spent much of the day on the telephone to Truman and Stalin but by the early evening had yielded to the inevitable – VE Day would be set for Tuesday 8 May.

Several miles from Downing Street, in a quintessentially English scene, a Mass-Observation interviewer chatted to a disgruntled neighbour over the runner bean poles of their allotments: 'Dick Masters was on his patch and said he was disappointed, as he had been expecting the same thing as I had done. We both felt that the whole thing was very confusing and poorly handled, and couldn't see any logical reason for the delay in giving the news ... I know in my

On VE-1 Princess Elizabeth fulfils her duties as Colonel-in-Chief of the Grenadier Guards by inspecting the 5th Battalion at Wellington Barracks, London.

own mind that the war in Europe *is* over, for all practical purposes, and I find it very confusing and perplexing.'

In a news bulletin at 3pm the BBC reported, without comment, Schwerin von Krosigk's broadcast to the German nation. For many this was the signal that the war was over. At Sissinghurst, his country home in Kent, Harold Nicolson was listening to the radio: '3pm and the news. It says that an hour ago Schwerin von Krosigk had spoken on the wireless from Flensburg. He has said that Germany was obliged to surrender unconditionally, crushed by the overwhelming might of her enemies. Ben [his son] and I dash off to tell Vita [Nicolson's wife, the writer Vita Sackville-West] in the courtyard. The three of us climb the turret stairs, tie the flag on to the ropes, and hoist it in the soft south-west breeze. It looks very proud and gay after five years of confinement.'

More exuberant souls sought a noisier release than the quietly deferred pleasures of Sissinghurst. The calm of London's Pimlico district, dozing in the afternoon sun, was shattered by the progress of a saloon car painted flaming red and equipped with a huge banner and loudspeaker, both of which proclaimed 'It's All Over'. In Dublin – where on 2 May Mr de Valera had expressed his condolences on Hitler's death to the German minister – a boisterous celebration by about 50 English students on the roof of the main entrance to Trinity College had boiled over into a general free-for-all when the crowd which had gathered below objected to the flying of the Irish tricolour below the Union Jack. Fighting spilled out over College Green and into Dame Street and the police were called in to quell a minor riot. Later, after a brawl outside the Wicklow Hotel, a large crowd marched down Nassau Street to the famous Jammet's restaurant, where they threw stones at the windows and sang several rousing choruses of the Soldiers Song in Irish before being dispersed by the police.

In Accrington, Lancashire, where folk are not usually given to sudden explosions of spontaneous emotion, the townspeople were torn between a desire to let out the pent-up tension and their commonsense feeling that the time to do so was when Mr Churchill made an official announcement. In the town centre, corporation workmen had made an early appearance, erecting scaffolding from the top of which they unfurled long strings of bunting. Small knots of people gathered to watch them at their work, setting up loudspeakers and floodlights in front of the Town Hall. There was an excited buzz of conversation – 'Had the council heard something?', 'Why were decorations being put up if nothing had been heard?'

Similar scenes, although on a much larger scale, were taking place in London outside Buckingham Palace. During the afternoon thousands of people had gathered outside the railings, scanning the windows of the Palace for the slightest sign of movement and watching workmen laying a carpet and sawing a platform on the balcony from which the King and Queen were to appear. At about 6.30pm one of the workmen at the Palace gate gave a shrug of his shoulders, a gesture of disappointment which communicated itself to the crowd. He and his mate clambered down their ladders, from which they had been fixing loudspeakers. Slowly the crowd began to melt away, leaving behind two young girls in paper hats perched defiantly on the Victoria Memorial.

In Trafalgar Square the attention of the quiet throng milling around the fountains was suddenly caught by a rumbling noise approaching from the Strand. As they craned their necks for a better view, a long line of students from University College burst into the square bearing their mascot 'Phineas' in the front rank of the procession and singing, 'Oh, Why Are We Waiting?' to the tune of 'Oh, Come All Ye Faithful'. Still singing, they disappeared in the direction of Whitehall.

Outside London the early evening passed quietly. A Chepstow woman visiting Bristol wrote in her diary: 'The same crowds were bustling home from work, as it is now 5pm, and stood patiently in queues looking as if their only aim in life at the moment is to get home as quickly as possible after a day's toil.' A young woman who had spent much of the war as an Air Raid Warden in the Midlands went to a Wardens' party at her local pub, The Wooden Post: 'The pub was as quiet as a church – at least for about the first hour. We sat around drinking mild on a very modest scale, exchanged reminiscences about the Blitz, deplored the Polish deadlock, refused to buy some very shoddy red white and blue favours which were being hawked around by an Asiatic (there is a colony in this neighbourhood) ... People were singing songs of the last war, but in a rather laboured and not very spontaneous way.'

IT'S OFFICIAL

Finally, at 7.40pm, the Ministry of Information threw its overmastering caution to the winds and issued a statement on the radio. Remarkably, it succeeded in falling as flat as Neville Chamberlain's querulous declaration of war six years before on 3 September 1939: 'It is understood that, in accordance with arrangements between the three great powers, an official announcement will be broadcast by the Prime Minister at three o'clock tomorrow, Tuesday afternoon, 8 May. In view of this fact, tomorrow, Tuesday, will be treated as Victory-in-Europe Day, and will be regarded as a holiday. The day following, Wednesday 9 May, will also be a holiday. His Majesty the King will broadcast to the people of the British Empire and Commonwealth, tomorrow, Tuesday, at 9pm.' Thus, in the nannyish, pedantic tones of a civil servant, was the news of VE Day brought to the British people.

In a quiet London suburb the news flash was heard by a commercial artist, at home alone with his children while his wife was on part-time duty at the local telephone exchange: 'So tomorrow is VE Day. I heard the news flash ... and went out to see whether anyone else had heard it. A youngster across the street shouted the news to me, not excited, just glad, and he finished, "I suppose that means we don't go into work tomorrow – that suits me fine". There were very few flags out in this street at the time, and I immediately went up and put up my own, a Union Jack and a rather old South African flag ... I don't think that the rest of the street had heard the announcement, so at nine I put the radio on at full blast and opened all the windows. Heads came up, spades went down and the whole neighbourhood went indoors. Bedroom windows began to pop open, and within a quarter of an hour some dozens of flags had been put up. On the average there is only one flag per house, but a few have two or three. I cannot say I am wildly excited ... Just a pleasant feeling of "Well, that's over – what now?".'

The 9pm announcement was the signal which nudged most of Britain from uncertainty into celebration. Across the Channel in Paris, bedlam had reigned all day as, in the words of the New York Herald Tribune, 'hundreds of thousands of Parisians jammed into the streets, pistols were fired into the air from moving cars, planes overhead dropped multicolored flares and fireworks boomed in all directions.' In Lübeck, on the Baltic, which had fallen to the British on 2 May, the photo-journalist Margaret Bourke-White found parties everywhere on 7 May: '...the streets were full of merry Englishmen driving fantastically luxurious motor cars, which Wehrmacht officers had abandoned along the roads – red-upholstered Mercedes Benzes, Hispanos, Renaults and other top-drawer limousines... The British supplied ... dress swords by the bucketful for anyone who wanted German souvenirs.'

Now, in their own fashion, the British began to make up for lost time. The restless crowds which had dispersed three hours earlier were soon back in the streets of central London. In Trafalgar Square a double decker bus inched through the crush carrying a platoon of soldiers on its roof. At the Cambridge Circus end of Shaftesbury Avenue an old hurdy gurdy was set up. Two middle-aged women twirled about it and, whenever the opportunity arose, hitched up their skirts and showed their bloomers amid roars of approval from all around. In Leicester Square and Piccadilly Circus press photographers and agency cameramen were at work, urging the crowd – many of whom still looked more bewildered than exultant – to 'look up!' at the sunburst of popping flash bulbs.

In a report filed with Mass-Observation a young London woman painted a vivid picture of the events of the evening and the mood of the period. Passing by bonfires in Piccadilly Circus and Coventry Street, she joined a long queue for a Lyons Corner House. The flames from the Coventry Street bonfire illuminated a large street-level hoarding advertising a James Mason-Margaret Lockwood film, *A Place of One's Own*, and the latest offering from Rita Hayworth. From this vantage point she watched sparks from the bonfire whirling skywards as it was fed with timber from a nearby bomb-site. The queue shuffled forward at an agonizingly slow-pace – after nearly two hours our Mass-Observer noted that she had progressed from the large image of James Mason at one end of the poster to Margaret Lockwood at the other end. The people in the queue – most of them couples – diverted themselves with a great deal of 'furtive kissing in dark corners', while an Army officer suggested feeding the blaze with the wooden shutters from the Corner House, which were propped up against a wall. No sooner had this been done than a fire engine arrived to douse the flames to the accompaniment of cheerful cries of 'spoilsports'. As the onset of rain completed the firemen's task, a French tank corps man planted a big kiss full on the Mass-Observer's lips. Behind her in the queue a solitary soldier raised the pathetic cry, 'Everybody's got a girl but me.' As the crowd rekindled the embers of the bonfire a man's voice called out, 'Rita Hayworth, you're going to have your legs scorched by the morning.' After another visit from the Auxiliary Fire Service the crowd around the bonfire drifted away, leaving the queue for the Corner House to their seemingly endless vigil. It was not until the small hours that the Mass-Observer finally got inside, only to find herself at the back of another queue. There is more than a hint of wartime stoicism in her laconic comment, 'But at least it was dry.'

As midnight approached, a young housewife went up to the roof of her flat on London's Edgware Road, '...from which my husband and I have so often watched fires flaring up in a ring around London as far as we could see, and seen explosions, listened to bombs and 'planes and guns during the "Little Blitz" of spring '44: also watched buzz bombs with their flaring tails careering along over the houses before the final "bang"...As I looked, fireworks began to erupt around the horizon and the red glow of distant bonfires lit the sky – peaceful and joyous fires, now, in place of the terrifying ones of the last years.'

VE DAY

As midnight struck on 7 May the big ships riding at anchor in ports from the Firth of Clyde to Southampton opened up their sirens in deep-throated, booming V signals. Smaller craft followed them with a cacophony of hoots and whistles and searchlights flashed out a V in Morse across the sky. The noise could be heard for miles inland, and people living on the coast, thrilled by the din, defied the continuing blackout regulations, threw open their curtains and let their lights blaze out into the night.

In London VE Day arrived in equally dramatic fashion. In the small hours a massive thunderstorm raged, reminding Londoners of the great storm which had burst over the capital on the last night of peace, 2 September 1939, and also providing an echo of the Blitz of 1940. One person who was not disturbed by the thunder was Winston Churchill, who was up till nearly 4am dictating to his secretary. Later she recalled, 'Once or twice he said with a twinkle, "What was that? Oh, only thunder", or "Might as well be another war".' Not everyone was so sanguine. In a final sideswipe at the bungling of the authorities a Bicester woman wrote in her diary, 'Precisely at midnight ... a violent thunderstorm. It seems as if the clerk of the weather had better and more striking ideas of marking victory than the human authorities.'

By 7am, when Stuart Hibberd read the first news bulletin of the day, the storm had exhausted itself, leaving behind an overcast sky fitfully pierced by the sun. Among the principal items in the news were the King's message of congratulation to General Eisenhower; the liberation of King Leopold of the Belgians by the US 7th Army; the drive in the Far East for Okinawa and the battle for Borneo; and in Europe the surrender of Breslau to the Russians. Main-line railway services were promised for VE Day, with the addition of special late relief trains. On VE Day+1 a Sunday train service was planned. London Transport was to provide a Sunday service on both days. In order to prevent half the capital's buses, trams and trolley buses from being engulfed in the West End celebrations, it was announced that they would 'leave the central area earlier than on ordinary days'. In a pointed effort to avoid hopelessly clogged switchboards, the Post Office announced that they were suspending cheap night telephone calls and cutting back on the telegraph service.

For Daily Mirror readers there was a long-awaited pleasure to savour over the breakfast table – the final unveiling of the scantily clad cartoon strip heroine Jane in all her naked splendour. Events had overtaken the paper's promise to reveal all on the day of victory, and as a result the strip's storyline had mysteriously lurched forward several days.

The journalist Tom Pocock recalled that the mood on the morning of VE Day was 'quiet at first and meditative, sometimes close to silent tears'. For many the meditating was done in yet more queues. At the moment of victory the shortages began to bite deeper. In the Surrey town of Dorking one of the Mass-Observation team noted, '8.30am – crowds lined up at bakeries, the first time I had seen this since the New Year Fire Blitz. There is not nearly enough bread to go round.' Alcohol was also in short supply: 'All the provisions shops were open and were crowded ... as much as £4 was being offered for gin and whisky, but there was none for sale.' A London woman wrote in her diary, 'May 8, Tuesday, a thunderstorm greeted VE Day, but was over before I went to join the longest fish queue I can remember.'

above Comic-strip heroine Jane disrobed at last for Daily Mirror readers on VE Day.

left Decorated for the occasion, Evening News vans wait to rush their first VE Day editions on to the streets of London.

There was still a lingering testiness with the confused way in which the war had come to an end. One Mass-Observer overheard a conversation in a small newsagent's which would have been worthy of Harold Pinter. A middle-aged woman opened the exchange, determined to make the most of that great British tradition – moaning.

'They played us a dirty trick – a proper dirty trick.' A young labourer chipped in, 'A muddle it was – just a muddle.' Then a young woman took up the refrain, 'People waiting and waiting and nothing happening. No church bells or nothing'. The labourer's companion, a man of about 50, joined in, 'Yes – what 'appened to them church bells, I'd like to know! Well I'm sick and tired – browned off with 'em, I am. The way they've behaved – why it was an insult to the people. Stood up to all wot we've stood up to, and then afraid to tell us it was peace, just as if we were a lot of kids. Just as if we couldn't be trusted to behave ourselves ... It should have been yesterday, when you think of it – peace was signed at 2.40 in the morning, and then people wait and wait all day .... No bells, no all-clears, nothing to start people off.' At which point the instigator of the conversation rounded it off triumphantly, if somewhat cryptically, with 'That's just what they're afraid of, I reckon.'

There was still a tentative mood hanging over London. The writer John Lehmann recalled, 'My chief recollection of VE Day is of queuing for a bus to Paddington that never came, and finally having to walk right across Hyde Park with a heavy suitcase in one hand and a briefcase in the other, pouring with sweat. The crowds were more dazed than excited, and they seemed to gather more and more, in a slow groundswell, no wild battering of waves, good-tempered, a little bewildered and awkward about celebrating, like cripples taking their first steps after a miraculous healing, not fully grasping yet the implications of the new life ahead of them. Now the noise of the last all-clear on the sirens seemed to prolong itself in the mind's ear until it was beyond the range of hearing forever.'

THE CROWDS GATHER

Strolling through Mayfair to the Ritz, Sir Henry 'Chips' Channon, the Conservative MP and arch-appeaser of the pre-war years, found the streets 'almost empty'. However, by lunchtime the West End had begun to fill up. In Trafalgar Square the newly erected boards around the base of Nelson's column read 'Victory over Germany 1945' and, rather more optimistically, 'Give Thanks by Saving'. Outside the National Gallery a cluster of hawkers had erected their own signs: 'God Has Been Good To Us, It's Up To Us Now', and 'There'll Always Be An England – We have Beaten Them Three Times Including Once at Tottenham', a reference to a pre-war soccer international at White Hart Lane. One florid-faced hawker was selling Churchill buttonhole badges, calling out, 'Churchill for sixpence! Worth More!' Around the salesmen milled a cheerful throng, almost all of them sporting a variety of Victory favours in red white and blue, including rosettes emblazoned with 'Adolf, You've Had It', 'Thanks, Monty' and 'Kiss Me, Darling'. One small boy was spotted wearing a sweater covered with the names of Allied generals, prominent among which were Montgomery, Eisenhower and Patton. A bus passed by on which someone had chalked in huge letters, 'This Is The Bus That Hitler Missed'.

Harold Nicolson had lunched at the Beefsteak. His diary does not record the bill of fare, but had he lunched at the Savoy he could have enjoyed *La Tasse de Consommé Niçoise de la Victoire, La Volaille des*

Crowds stream past the Cenotaph in Whitehall while more intrepid souls view the proceedings from the roof of a ministry building.

WHEN THE LIGHTS GO ON AGAIN

Iles Britanniques, La Citronette Joyeuse Délivrance, La Coupe Glacée des Alliés and *Le Médaillon du Soldat*. When he re-emerged, to walk down to Parliament Square, the quiet Bank Holiday scene had been transformed: 'I find the streets very crowded and people wearing all manner of foolish paper caps and cheering slightly. When I leave the club at 2.15, I find the roads packed. Trafalgar Square is a seething mass of people with figures draped over the lions. Whitehall is overflowing, but a few buses try to push their way through. After the Cenotaph it is just a jam. I squeeze in behind a car and manage to reach the House at about 5 to three. I pause to recover myself in Palace Yard and regret to observe that I have torn a hole in my new suit.'

CHURCHILL'S DAY

The moment was approaching when Churchill would speak to the nation from Downing Street. Inside No 10 the staff gathered outside the door of the cabinet room as the Prime Minister prepared to go on the air. According to his secretary, Elizabeth Nel, 'Just before three we heard a great trumpeting sound over the loudspeaker as he blew his nose, then some remarks, "Pull down that blind", "What are you doing with that?" ... "Move a little further away please", but of course ... he was not yet on the air.'

In Parliament Square the sun broke through as the moment arrived.

right Time for a snack in Piccadilly Circus.

far right The army and navy join the crowd in giving this young airman his own accolade outside Buckingham Palace.

below right Revellers take a truck ride through Parliament Square as the growing crowd waits to hear Churchill's speech.

below The flags may all have gone at Derry & Toms but on the streets hawkers were still hoping to make a last-minute sale.

WHEN THE LIGHTS GO ON AGAIN

Big Ben chimed the hour and Churchill's voice was carried loud and clear over the upturned faces of the crowd and beyond them across Britain. His speech was short, sturdy and effective: 'Yesterday at 2.41am the representative of the German High Command and government, General Jodl, signed the act of unconditional surrender of all German land, sea and air forces in Europe, to the Allied Expeditionary Force and to the Soviet High Command. Today this agreement will be ratified and confirmed at Berlin ... Hostilities will end officially at one minute after midnight tonight, Tuesday, 8 May, but in the interests of saving lives the "Cease Fire" began yesterday to be sounded along the fronts ... The German war is therefore at an end. Our gratitude to all our splendid allies goes forth from all our hearts in this Island and the British Empire.

'We may allow ourselves a brief period of rejoicing but let us not forget for a moment the toils and efforts that lie ahead. Japan, with all her treachery and greed, remains unsubdued. The injustices she has inflicted upon Great Britain and the United States, and other countries, and her detestable cruelties, call for justice and retribution. We must now devote all our strength and resources to the completion of our task both at home and abroad. Advance Britannia! Long live the cause of freedom! God save the King!'

The thousands in Parliament Square listened intently, raising a mighty roar when Churchill announced that from midnight hostilities were to cease, and another to greet the news that at the same time the Channel Islands were to be liberated. There were whoops of joy and flags waved when he came to the point in his speech at which he declared, 'The German war is therefore at an end'. As Churchill finished, the buglers of the Royal Horse Guards sounded the Cease Fire. Then, as the haunting notes died away, the band struck up 'God Save the King'. Soldiers and civilians alike stood smartly to attention and sang the National Anthem with a fervour which reminded one observer of the singing of a 'sacred hymn'.

It was, perhaps, a sign of the shift in the wind that Churchill's speech did not impress everyone who heard it. A Chepstow diarist recorded, 'So very little indication that a momentous event in history was taking place. People in the street went on their way undisturbed and no one stopped beside the open window to listen to the radio which could have been heard.' The writer John Grigg thought the speech little more than 'ham' and even the faithful Lord Moran, Churchill's personal physician, felt that it had a 'tinny sound'. The element of theatricality which had been so spellbinding in the war – with its studied mis-pronunciation of German names, in this case that of the hapless Jodl – was to exercise a waning appeal in time of peace. A serviceman in Holland observed, 'At the moment of final victory British soldiers ... were seen to mimic the cadences once thought so rousing and now felt to be behind the times.' For some, the arrival of peace had already provided a dramatic change in perspective. After the German surrender in Italy, Geoffrey Cox, an intelligence officer serving with the New Zealand division, looked up and saw his fellow officers in a completely different light: 'In the mess the extravagant, unorthodox garb which, in the days of battle, had added a dashing cavalier touch to these officers ... now seemed affected if not effete. One officer wore a neck scarf of vivid carnation and gold; another had a coat with a white fur collar. His black hair was, by military standards, very long; a great white hound lay at his feet. Their easy bantering manner, so valuable as a counter to tension in hard fighting times, now seemed out of touch with the world.'

Churchill with service chiefs in the sunny garden of 10 Downing Street on the morning of VE Day.

Churchill engulfed by crowds as he makes his way to the Palace.

Nevertheless, on 8 May Churchill could bask in the glow of victory. It was to remain his day. After taking leave of his personal staff, he proceeded by car to the Houses of Parliament. The crush in Whitehall was by now so great that the car was propelled along by the enthusiastic crowd, each one eager to catch a glimpse of the great man. Churchill's slow, triumphal progress now created a technical hitch at the Commons, for by 3.15 Question Time had finished and the Prime Minister was still not in his place. Everyone's eyes were on the door behind the Speaker's chair. It was left to the author and wit A.P. Herbert to fill the gap with an arcane Parliamentary fiction. He rose to ask the Leader of the House when the government proposed to proceed with the Outlawries Bill which was 'formally read at the beginning of each Session ... to preserve the right of members to discuss what they will'. The ensuing exchange was spun out over the next eight minutes, at which point Churchill made his entrance from behind the Speaker's Chair. Harold Nicolson watched him as he entered the chamber: 'I see a stir at the door and Winston comes in – a little shy – a little flushed – but smiling boyishly.' He was greeted with ecstatic cheering and the wild waving of order papers. Everyone rose to their feet, save the Russian ambassador and, according to Chips Channon, 'the recently elected cad from Chelmsford'. Even the normally blasé regulars in the Press gallery stood up and added their 'Hurrahs' to the din. Churchill acknowledged the applause with 'an odd, shy jerk of the head and a wide grin'. He repeated the short statement he had made from Downing Street and then, 'with more gesture and emphasis than is customary to him', he thanked the House for its support throughout the conflict. Then he begged to move 'That this House do now attend at the Church of St Margaret, Westminster, to give humble and reverent thanks to Almighty God for our deliverance from the threat of German domination".'

The procession was led by the Speaker, magnificent in his Court Robes, and the Serjeant at Arms, also in full dress and carrying the

Mr and Mrs Cooper and family
tune in their wireless set to listen
to Churchill's speech.

mace. Behind them came the Chaplain, the Prime Minister, the acting
leader of the Labour Party Arthur Greenwood, then the Privy
Councillors in groups of four, and finally the MPs walking two
abreast. Slowly they filed out by St Stephen's entrance through a lane
in the crowd kept open by the police. Harold Nicolson noted, 'The
crowd are friendly, recognizing some of the members. I am with
Nancy Astor who is, I feel, a trifle hurt that she does not get more
cheering.'

Tom Driberg, then the Independent Labour MP for Maldon, has left
an account of the service: 'The windows of the church were still drably
darkened; but the violet gown of the Speaker's chaplain ... caught the
eye vividly as he stood before the blushing peonies and azaleas
massed on the altar. The service had an almost Presbyterian flavour,
a restrained dignity ... The singing was rich and exultant. The
dramatic climax was the end; the organ was playing, the west doors
were flung open, the warm, living sunshine poured in, there was a
second of suspense – and then, simultaneously, the bells pealed out
clamorously, rocking the roof above us, and the crowds cheered
wildly as they saw the Speaker and the Prime Minister emerging.'

For Harold Nicolson, 'The supreme moment is when the Chaplain
reads out the names of those members of Parliament who have lost
their lives. It is a sad thing to hear. My eyes fill with tears. I hope that
Nancy does not see, "Men are so emotional", she says.'

On the walk back to the Houses of Parliament, Churchill was again
almost engulfed by people running, standing on tiptoe to glimpse
him, or holding up babies so that years hence they could be told that
they had seen him. From all sides the cry went up, 'Winnie, Winnie!'
One battered old cockney woman, clearly happily sozzled, bawled
out, 'That's 'im, that's 'is little old lovely bald head.' There was
another act of lèse majesté as Churchill re-entered the Houses of

The dense crowd outside the Palace shortly before Churchill emerged.

Parliament. A small boy (Master Peter Bland of Golders Green), who had been pursuing Churchill all the way back from St Margaret's church, finally caught up with him on the threshold of the members' lobby and asked him for his autograph. He was not to be denied. After two refusals Churchill solemnly took off his glasses, ruffled the lad's hair and signed his book, observing, 'That will remind you of a glorious day.'

This, however, was only the beginning of Churchill's day. At 4pm he drove to Buckingham Palace, diverting on the way to reclaim his cigar case which he had absent-mindedly left behind at No 10 Downing Street. As he told his detective, the crowd would have felt cheated if he did not appear with this familiar prop. With his unfailing sense of theatre, he paused on the steps of No 10 to light up a Havana before moving on to his car. Shortly afterwards he appeared with the

Churchill with the Royal Family on the balcony of Buckingham Palace in the afternoon.

Royal Family on the balcony at Buckingham Palace. The King was bare-headed and wearing a naval uniform; Her Majesty was dressed in blue, as was the 14-year-old Princess Margaret; Princess Elizabeth appeared in her uniform of second subaltern of the ATS.

An hour later a massive crowd had gathered below the windows of the Ministry of Health building in Whitehall from which, the word had spread, Churchill was to deliver another speech. The minutes ticked away. Occasionally a brave soul shinned up a lamp post or a bus stop sign, the latter an excruciatingly uncomfortable perch. There were sporadic bursts of cheering from the crowd – 'We Want Winnie! We Want Winnie!' A voice from the back of the crowd yelled, 'Why don't 'e come out?', only to receive the ironic reply,' 'E's 'aving a drink, dear.' An expertly fashioned paper 'plane flew out of one of the upper windows and swooped over the crowd. Heads strained to watch its flight and hands reached up to grasp it as it slowly descended. Someone remarked, 'I've never seen one better made. Leonardo must have been about somewhere.' As the hands of the clock crept round to 6 o'clock an old, cracked female voice called out, with unconscious irony, 'Come on, Winnie. We shan't want you for long.' At last, to a terrific burst of cheering, Churchill appeared on the balcony puffing a cigar. As he gave the V sign the crowd roared itself hoarse. Then he addressed the crowd: 'This is your victory. It is the victory of the cause of freedom in every land. In all our long history we have never seen a greater day than this. Everyone, man or woman, has done their best. Everyone has tried. Neither the long years, nor the dangers, nor the fierce attacks of the enemy, have in any way weakened the deep resolve of the British nation. God bless you all.'

Artist Leila Faithfull's impression of the view from Green Park towards the Palace.

A mother and her son walk back towards Trafalgar Square after the long wait outside the Palace.

As soon as Churchill disappeared inside the Ministry of Health the crowd began to disperse with uncanny orderliness, so ingrained had become the wartime habit of queuing. Four hours later, when Churchill returned for more speeches, the crowd in Whitehall was in a more boisterous mood. Surrounded by members of the wartime government, Churchill drank in the applause. Seizing the moment, Ernest Bevin stepped forward to call for three cheers for victory and then led the crowd in singing 'For He's A Jolly Good Fellow'. To Churchill's detective the Prime Minister seemed 'like a schoolboy on an outing'. His secretary Elizabeth Nel watched him intently throughout the performance: 'I shall always remember Mr Churchill as he was at that moment, spick and span in black and white striped trousers, a flower in his buttonhole, his face smooth and pink, a man of medium height and somewhat round of figure ... That was Mr Churchill's hour ... He knew so well what to say.' Now Churchill was conducting an intimate conversation with the 30,000 people massed below the balcony and stretching all the way from the Cenotaph to the House of Commons. They were in the palm of his hand, eagerly responding to all his cues: 'We were the first, in this ancient land, to draw the sword against Germany. After a while we were left alone against the most tremendous military power that has been seen. We were all alone for a whole year. There we stood. Did anyone want to give in? Were we downhearted?' As Churchill, now in full flow, declared, 'The lights went out and the bombs came down', the floodlighting momentarily flickered off, sending gales of ribald laughter rippling through the crowd. Churchill brought what was in effect his last 'wartime' speech to a close on a rousing note: 'When shall the reputation and faith of this generation of English men and women fail? I say that in the long years to come not only the people of this island, but from all over the world, wherever the bird of freedom chirps in human hearts, they will look back to what we have done, and they will say, "Don't despair, don't yield to violence and tyranny. March straight forward, and die, if need be, unconquered."' As the cheering died away, Churchill led the crowd in singing 'Land of Hope and Glory'.

THE KING'S SPEECH

At 9pm the King had made the other keynote speech of the day. It was one of his longest, lasting 13 minutes, and all who listened had his painful stammer uppermost in their minds, a handicap which increased their identification with him. Here is a typical reaction, from a woman who had spent the war producing educational film-strips: 'At 9pm the King. Most people that I know seem to feel the same about his speeches. Admiration for the way he faces his difficulties, fear that he shall trip up, and a kind of personal embarrassment when he seems likely to do so. I'm afraid it rather distracts from his matter sometimes, but it can't be helped and, anyway, it gives an impression of common humanity which no oratory can do. Pity, though, for he has, otherwise, a fine resonant voice reminiscent of his father's. A good speech, but unnecessarily formal. The occasion demanded it, and I do not expect he dare allow himself the luxury of emotion.'

Canadian soldiers entertain the public in Leicester Square while awaiting the broadcast of the King's speech.

A NIGHT OF REVELRY

By the early evening in central London, the feeling of being in an immense crowd bent on celebrating peace had begun to generate a real excitement. Even so, it was often left to the extroverts to play the principal roles. The great majority were content to sing and cheer when they were told to, and to admire the antics of less self-conscious revellers as they cavorted in the unfamiliar brightness of the floodlighting and cinema and theatre illuminations. Tom Driberg was watching the scene: 'In the orange glow that streamed down from the

Tivoli to the pavement of the Strand, a buxom woman in an apron made of a Union Jack, and a man of respectable middle-class appearance, did an exaggeratedly Latin-American dance while an accordion played "South of the Border"... As I picked my unobtrusive way along Coventry Street, a cheerful woman bawled, "MPs – yer off duty tonight!" I started guiltily: but she was addressing two Redcaps [military policemen]. On the roof above Scott's dignified oyster house an airman and a Yank did a fantastic Harold Lloyd act, elaborately sharing a bottle, tossing coins down to the people, who screamed each time they swayed over the parapet...'

In Piccadilly Circus the urban mountaineers had been quicker off the mark. At midday, a young man in the black beret of the Tank Corps was the first to scramble up the protective pyramidal structure erected early in the war to shield Eros' pedestal after the statue had been removed. Balanced at the top, he assumed on tiptoe an approximation of the Eros pose, aiming an imaginary bow. He was quickly followed by a paratrooper in a maroon beret who hauled up after him an attractive young blonde woman. She was promptly grabbed by the Tank Corps man, who seemed determined to act out the classic role of Eros in full view of everyone in Piccadilly Circus. But a moment later he was joined by several GIs, and in a matter of minutes the pyramid was covered with a mass of people sitting jammed together in a carefree jumble, exchanging uniform caps with each other and wisecracks with the crowd, one of whom observed, 'My God – think of a flying bomb coming down on this'.

As darkness fell in Piccadilly a sailor stripped off his clothes and, sporting a placard proclaiming 'Sold Out', joined the crowd on the Eros pyramid. An American serviceman, not to be outdone, climbed a lamp post and treated the crowd to an impromptu striptease, tossing down items of uniform one by one until he was left in his underpants. Another intrepid band had clambered on to the roof of a shelter in Piccadilly Circus. Among them was a young woman who at some point in the evening had been separated from her skirt and was now clutching a short raincoat around her. A searchlight was feeling its way around the Circus and suddenly struck the group, isolating the girl in the middle of its glare. The beam lingered for some time, and as one observer recalled, 'You should have heard the crowd cheer – they nearly went mad!'

In Trafalgar Square a huge throng around the plinth of Nelson's column were entertained by two Bevin Boys, who sang 'the Bevin Song' and recited 'The Boy Stood on the Burning Deck', during which one of them lost his footing and plunged dramatically into the crowd below. Scrambling back, he informed them, 'I was overcome with emotion.' Standing at the edge of one of the fountains in the square was a pretty girl in a red frock decorated with big white polka dots. She was amusing herself by teasing three rather stuffy-looking officers of the Norfolk Regiment. Hitching up her skirt, she waded into the water, gamely followed by the officers, who had prudently rolled up their trousers as if for a paddle at the seaside. All four climbed to the top of the fountain where, with heavy gallantry, they each gave the girl a kiss. A cameraman from Movietone News was on hand to film their descent, and as they splashed down in the pool at the base of the fountain the girl flipped up her skirts and exclaimed, 'I've never shown so much leg in my life!' She was borne off on the shoulders of one of the officers as the crowd sang 'For She's a Jolly Good Fellow'. As she wobbled out of view, a middle-aged woman remarked tartly, 'I'll bet she'll cop it when her mother sees it on the pictures.'

Students add an element of rag to the celebrations in central London.

With the waiting and the formalities over, Londoners threw restraint to the winds as evening approached.

The war gave a new sense of independence to young women in Britain. Their mood of relaxed confidence on VE night was noted by a Manchester Guardian correspondent.

left Land Army girls out to enjoy themselves in Trafalgar Square.

right Wrens dancing their way up Whitehall.

below A fine array of Victory favours in Piccadilly Circus.

That night there seemed a relaxed liberation from pre-war constraint among many young women. A Manchester Guardian correspondent noted the 'curious' fact of 'the number of parties of young girls without a man among them walking along the streets and singing. Many of them have been in the ATS or the WAAF and one noticed a large group of Land Army Girls in shirts and breeches singing their way along Oxford Street. There have been other parties of girls, too, who were not in uniform, some of them young clerks or typists, others apparently of the upper-middle classes, but quite content to amuse themselves in their own way without any help from the men ... No doubt uniformed service has produced in many girls a group spirit and a new feeling of their value and independence as women. As for the non-uniformed girls, one contributing cause may be that so many more of them are now economically independent and have got into the habit of looking after themselves.' Nevertheless, on VE Day many women looked forward to the restoration of a more traditional order. Writing in the progressive magazine Leader, Lesley Storm eagerly anticipated the return of men from war service with their 'restless masculinity around the house again – noisy, over-exuberant, careless and forever hungry ... Cigarette ends burning themselves out on the mantelpiece. The bathroom floor swimming in water with the towels making soggy islands in the middle.'

Just as it had been the day before, Buckingham Palace was the focus of activity in central London. Thousands of people had milled about in front of the railings all day, cheering virtually everything

that moved, including the memorably Edwardian sight of a bearded army officer arriving for an investiture in an old horse cab which clumped along with an aged cabby in a billycock. After the King's broadcast at 9pm, the waiting crowd took up the strains of 'For He's a Jolly Good Fellow' and 'Land of Hope and Glory'. There was a sudden hush as lights came on in the room behind the balcony in Buckingham Palace, then a storm of cheering as the floodlights were switched on. 'He's coming, he's coming' was on everyone's lips. At last the Royal Family appeared on the balcony. When they slipped back inside the Palace a huge sigh of disappointment ran through the crowd, instantly stilled when they came out again. The Royal Family returned another six times, 'just like a cuckoo clock', as someone in the crowd remarked, and it was nearly 11pm before they went inside for the last time. It was then that the King allowed the two princesses, accompanied by two young officers, to see the sights outside the Palace. They mingled with the crowd and, according to Princess Margaret, 'Everyone was knocking off each other's hats, and we knocked off some too.' Later that night the King struck a tender and slightly melancholy note in his diary when he wrote, 'Poor darlings, they have never had any fun yet.'

Among the crowd outside Buckingham Palace was a young Guards officer, Humphrey Lyttelton. Flushed with a champagne supper in St James Park, he produced a trumpet, gathered a raggle taggle band around him and, mounted on a handcart, led a huge swaying conga chain of revellers to Trafalgar Square and then back to the Palace. Lyttelton recalled, as the Royal Family appeared on the balcony, 'I dimly remember blasting a chorus of "For He's a Jolly Good Fellow" in the direction of His Majesty.'

Two's company, three's a crowd on a lamp standard in Piccadilly Circus.

Urban mountaineers on the statueless, boarded-up plinth of Eros in Piccadilly Circus.

As midnight approached inhibitions fell away.

WHEN THE LIGHTS GO ON AGAIN

As midnight approached, inhibitions fell away. It needed only one person to take the lead and very soon he had acquired hundreds of eager followers. In Leicester Square a sprucely dressed officer from a Highland Regiment, clanging away at two dustbin lids, was at the head of a long procession which stretched back for 100 yards. One of the Mass-Observation team watched a young woman, arm-in-arm with a sailor, walk up to a policeman and, blowing a streamer in his face, sing in a slightly tipsy voice, 'If You Want to Know the Time, Ask a Policeman'. The policeman turned to the sailor and in a very matter-of-fact voice – as if he was supplying street directions – said, 'Look after her, sailor boy'.

There was very little drunkenness on VE night, nor any of the wild copulation between total strangers which had been such a feature of the Armistice night celebrations in 1918. Most drunks were tolerantly left to their own devices. In Oxford Street a middle-aged labourer and a younger companion, both of them unable to walk straight, sat down on the white line in the middle of the road and remained there contentedly waving up at passing buses until they were gently moved on by a policeman. There was also a certain amount of lighthearted vandalism. A big, glowering bust of Mussolini was dragged out of the New Zealand Forces Club in the Charing Cross Road, and was soon being pelted with missiles. In Green Park someone who had failed to find a suitable flag was prancing about waving an enormous poster advertising Jeyes Disinfectant.

FIRES OF PEACE, MEMORIES OF WAR

Near the Ritz in Green Park was one of the thousands of bonfires which burned that night all over London and across the nation. James Lees-Milne watched the scene with an art historian's eye: 'In Green Park there was a huge bonfire under the trees, and too near one poor tree which caught fire.' Lees-Milne pushed through the crowd on the pavement and into the park 'to a ring of people round the bonfire. They were very funny, bringing huge posts from nowhere and hurling them on to the fire. Six or seven people were struggling under barricades of wood and whole doorways from air raid shelters which they dragged on to the fire. The fire's reflection on thousands of faces, packed on the pavement, squatting on the grass and cramming the windows of the Piccadilly houses, reminded me for some reason of a Harrison Ainsworth illustration of the crowds watching Charles I's execution. One extraordinary figure, a bearded naval titan, organized an absurd nonsense game, by calling out the Navy and making them tear round the bonfire carrying the Union Jack; then the RAF; then the Army; then the Land Army, represented by three girls only; then the Americans; then the civilians ... The scene was more Elizabethan than Georgian, a spontaneous peasant game, a dance around the maypole, almost Breughelian, infinitely bucolic.'

For others the fires reflected in the sky stirred more recent memories of the Blitz. The novelist William Sansom had spent the war as an auxiliary fireman and had played a leading role in the documentary *Fires Were Started*, Humphrey Jennings' moving tribute to the AFS: 'Pinpointed across the City [of Westminster] appeared the first urgent firebursts, ever growing, as though they were in fact spreading, as each bonfire reddened and cast its coppery glow on the house-rows, on glassy windows and the black blind spaces where windows had once been. Alleys lit up, streets took on the fireset glare – it seemed that in each dark declivity of houses there lurked the old fire. The ghosts of wardens and fireguards and firemen were felt scurrying

One of thousands of bonfires that burned in London that night – this one in Wapping in dockland.

A swaying line of conga dancers snakes past a London bonfire.

again down in the redness. Fireworks peppered the air with a parody of gunfire. The smell of burning wood charred the nostrils. And, gruesomely correct, some of the new street lights and fluorescent window lights ... glowed fiercely bluish-white, bringing again the shrill memory of the old white thermite glare of the bursting incendiary.'

Amid the rejoicing, VE night held its darker side. With a practised eye the homosexual Tom Driberg, an inveterate night-time cruiser, noticed, 'Here and there in sheltering darkness ... lonely living ghosts – a repatriated prisoner, dazed by the garish clamour and by the sudden accessibility of women after years of celibacy; a young American wounded in Germany and due for discharge, bitterly dreading his return to Maryland and the instability of civilian life.' Throughout Britain there were many foreign troops waiting to go back to their liberated – and devastated – homelands. The tubes and deep shelters still housed a permanent population of about 12,000 – people with seemingly nowhere else to go. The loss of family or friends also cast long shadows over the celebrations. A young woman who had been posted to Holland with the ATS wrote in her diary: 'This is at last VE Day. We are still operational as there is still fighting in Czechoslovakia and isolated places. Last night I heard that Jim [a close friend's husband] is "missing, believed killed", so I have not joined in the festive feeling ... Poor dear tenderhearted Jim. How true Frances was when she said in her letter that he was on his last trip ... I'm too sad to make this the entry I always intended.'

below and overleaf Floodlights illuminated many of London's historic buildings after years of blackout.

WHEN THE LIGHTS GO ON AGAIN

The floodlighting banished many of the shadows. If the crackling bonfires spoke of celebrations and battles which lay in the past, then the illumination of London's great buildings was for many a completely new phenomenon: Desmond McCarthey wrote, 'There was a new invention – floodlighting – which added to the dramatic beauty of the scene: London's finest buildings stood up white and dreamlike against the starry sky. The dome and cross of St Paul's looked in the distance like a marvellous piece of jewellery invented by a magician, while the Union Jack upon the dark Houses of Parliament, very faintly lit, curling and unfurling in the light wind, flickered like a mysterious and many-coloured flame.' Across the river County Hall was lit in two colours, and the training ships on the river strung with coloured lights. As the hands of Big Ben moved towards twelve there was a sudden hush in Parliament Square. At the last stroke of midnight a great cry went up – it was one minute past midnight, and the first day of peace.

below and right A selection of Victory souvenirs.

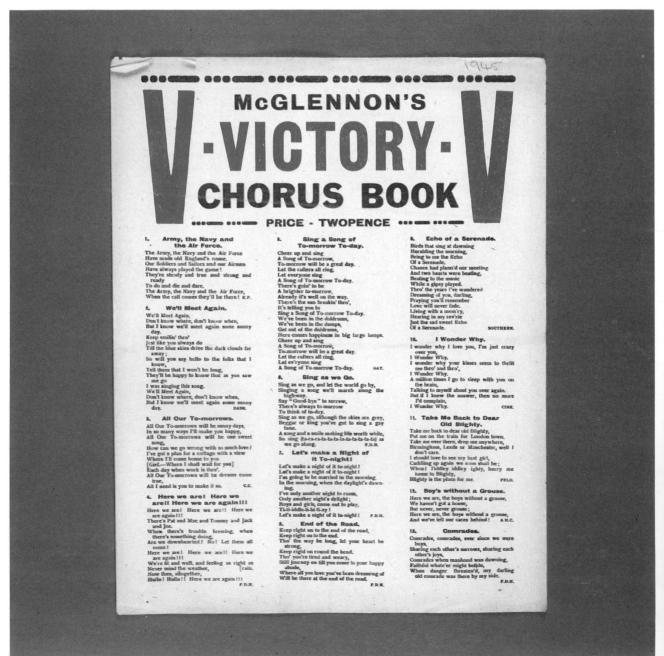

WHEN THE LIGHTS GO ON AGAIN

MEANWHILE, OUTSIDE LONDON...

Tom Pocock missed the transition from war to peace. Somewhat the worse for drink, he had taken a tumble, and on the morning of the 9th woke up to find himself between the crisp white sheets of a bed in St George's hospital. Inventing a cock and bull story about secret documents (Pocock was in Army intelligence) he retrieved his uniform and attempted to discharge himself. He was intercepted at the main entrance by a fearsome-looking matron, who escorted him to her office where his file was produced. To his shame, Pocock saw that he had been admitted a few minutes before midnight and entered on the records as a 'War Casualty'.

Outside the big focal points of central London the excitement had steadily fallen away. A member of the Mass-Observation team noted that at the top of Regent Street, 'people are now just walking in groups, as if it were a Sunday evening stroll in the park. A passing car, filled with Home Guard men, drops a thunder flash and roars off – something they couldn't have done in Piccadilly Circus.' In the suburbs the mood was one of dogged determination to celebrate rather than spontaneous rejoicing. A young soldier who in civilian life had been an articled clerk recorded his day in Pinner. It provides a fascinating insight into the public and private mood on VE Day. 'Crowds were wandering up and down the main street ... crowds going into church with the bell ringing. Even greater crowds somehow squashing into pubs. As it got dark, lights appeared outside shops – old neon signs, floodlighting on the church and the war memorial and crowds still wandering about just looking around and talking. Some Yanks passed through in a jeep throwing crackers about – an RAF officer lit some flares and parked them up on poles. About 11.30 the noise started. We had been invited into somebody's house and were indulging in some drinking. One of our party kept continually apologising for his "queer" behaviour (though it wasn't particularly queer) as he said that he has been in Germany until a few days back and was now on leave. He also keeps remarking, with obvious enjoyment, "I could go on with this for years, just loafing around doing nothing and enjoying myself." A party of people staggered up the road and then started singing – persistently – "Knees Up Mother Brown". Some lad climbed a lamp post and started playing accompaniments to the singing on an accordion. We played pontoon for a bit and listened to the late dance music. We finally left about 1.30 and started wandering home. Some chap was firing rockets in the main street and throwing crackers about. Still large crowds about. We went our various ways, everybody agreeing what a good evening it had been.'

While the rockets and flares fizzed up and down Pinner High Street a Buckinghamshire farmer and his wife strolled outside to gaze at the distant pink glow in the sky over London. The last time they had seen such a sight was at the height of the Blitz. Inevitably, the events in London on VE Day tended to overshadow the celebrations throughout the rest of the United Kingdom. But the day was one of national rejoicing, and in the regions people set about marking the occasion in their own ways. In the North and the Midlands the day got off to a damp start as the rain which had bucketed down on London in the small hours moved up through the country. The Accrington Times and Observer spoke of an 'impressive spectacle' in the Broadway as a big crowd listened to Churchill's speech. But the photograph on the front page reveals a sodden gathering – mostly women and children – shabby in their austerity clothing and huddled together against a background of flags tugged by a stiff breeze. It is a very English sight, and very affecting. Later, things brightened up in Accrington. From the early evening there was dancing in front of the Town Hall, where floodlights picked out a big silver V on the balcony, flanked by two silver doves of peace. Some of the town's young bloods amused themselves by throwing thunderflashes about, but there were no casualties. GIs from a nearby American camp gave a display of jitterbugging. The Times and Observer's dauntless reporter climbed on to the roof of a building overlooking the scene and spotted 'An old lady with silver hair and a red, white and blue skirt performing a jig to the accompaniment of handclapping.'

In Birmingham there were no fewer than eight services at the Cathedral, and at Aston Parish Church the crush of worshippers was so great that a service was provided on the hour every hour throughout the day. Secular forms of thanksgiving were on a more modest scale. The sober Birmingham Mail summed up the day in a commentary which catches the restrained spirit of austerity Britain, still unwilling or unable to let itself go. 'We are not much given to mass gaiety. We are gardeners, family men, artificers and very individualistic at that ... The war's hazards and chances will be lived again over drinks in the "local" as well as over high tea (or as "high" as we can make it) in the family parlour.' The editor then went on to make a positive virtue out of austerity: 'The illuminated tram and bus so widely advertised for our pleasure by indulgent City Fathers really are rather symptomatic of our mood. They will bring lights and glitter, and a whisper of glamour to our suburbs – and particularly the

St Paul's Cathedral looms through the shattered window of the Church of St Mary-le-Bow as its congregation gives thanks.

children – to save us a journey to the city. Just an ordinary tram and bus to begin with, but singled out from the other mass of trams and buses and made jubilant and individualistic. We can regard them as symbols of victory from a workaday world – yet give thanks that we don't have to travel in "lit up" buses and trams, or even blind ourselves by looking at them, every day of the week. The lights are no more than symbols. The real thing lies within.'

This philosophy of priggish restraint was evidently not shared by the raucous old lady who danced on the table tops of a genteel pub in Marlow, flashing her red, white and blue knickers at the patrons.

right Time for reflection as a lone sailor kneels in prayer in the bombed church of St Andrew, Plymouth.

below A Victory bell, made from melted down aircraft scrap.

WHEN THE LIGHTS GO ON AGAIN

Eventually she was ejected, but not all publicans were so flinty-hearted. At Burnham, in Buckinghamshire, one landlady kept her promise, made long before the end of the war, that if VE Day fell on her birthday she would put her stock of beer outside on the pavement for passers-by to help themselves. Many pubs were drunk dry on VE Day, but in Luton a sailor nobly attempted to make up for the shortage by dispensing beer to all-comers from a large bucket. In Plymouth another enterprising sailor was apprehended as he trundled along with a keg of beer liberated from the Avondale Arms Hotel. The next morning he was up before the Bench. The magistrate was in a lenient mood – 'A case of rolling out the barrel,' he remarked dryly before dismissing the case.

In some towns a hint of disgust with the defeated enemy lurked beneath the good-humoured surface. In Llanelly four German prisoners of war were spotted in a car, prompting a sudden barrage of fireworks and thunderflashes, one of which exploded inside the car, which drove off at great speed. In the Hampshire town of Andover a shop in Bridge Street sported an unusual decoration, a swastika flag which had been nailed to the bottom of the door. It was kicked, spat upon and eventually trampled underfoot by passers-by. By the early afternoon it had disappeared, with the exception of the torn ends which had not been ripped from the doorway. Flags, it seems, were items particularly at risk in the normally sleepy town of Andover. On VE Day+2 the local newspaper printed the following appeal: 'The Mayor has informed us that about midnight someone jumped up on the platform and slashed the Russian flag from off the Guildhall. No doubt it was done in a spirit of jollification, but he hopes that the flag will be returned to him as soon as possible.'

BONFIRES ACROSS BRITAIN

On VE Day most people's feelings about the Nazis were sublimated in the building of large bonfires, at the top of which were perched effigies of Hitler and his henchmen. Andover was no exception, and the inhabitants of that blameless community provided the Fuehrer's image with a pagan funeral pyre denied him in Berlin. As the local newspaper reported: 'From the centre of the pile rose a gibbet, and from it hung a very lifelike representation of the man who started the war. At a given signal children armed with lighted torches threw them into the pile which was soon a burning mass. Gradually the flames spread nearer and nearer to Hitler. Then his back began to blaze and, fanned by the slight breeze, he was quickly enveloped. It was not long before the rope by which he was attached to the scaffold burnt through and then, amid rousing cheers, he was engulfed in the flames.'

A correspondent in the Hereford Times wrote a graphic account of the bonfire in the small Herefordshire village of Stoke Lacy: 'Passing through the village of Stoke Lacy early on Tuesday afternoon one was startled to see an effigy of Hitler in the car park at the Plough. That evening a crowd began to gather, and word went round that Hitler was to be consumed in flames at 11pm. At that hour excitement was intense, when Mr W.R. Symonds called upon Mr S.J. Parker, the Commander of No 12 Platoon of the Home Guard, to set the effigy alight. In a few minutes the body of Hitler disintegrated as his 1,000 years empire had done. First his arm, poised in the Hitler salute, dropped as smartly as it was ever raised in life ... then a leg fell off, and the flames burnt fiercely to the strains of "Rule Britannia", "There'll Always be an England" and "Roll Out the Barrel". Then the crowd spontaneously linked hands and in a circle 300 strong sang

A children's Victory bonfire near Plymouth.

The people of Leeds drag a reluctant Hitler towards the bonfire.

128

WHEN THE LIGHTS GO ON AGAIN

"Auld Lang Syne". Mr Parker then called for cheers for Mr Churchill, President Truman, Marshal Stalin and our serving boys and girls. The ceremony was followed by the singing of "God Save the King".'

The bonfires frequently involved elaborate preparations and the events of the day – street parties, sports meetings and fancy dress parades – were organized around them. In Hanover Road, in north London, the community's young people gave the affair due publicity, making their own posters and setting them up at each end of the street. Small children were instructed to bring as many of their friends as they could, while the older boys made their own fireworks (a rather alarming undertaking). Everybody had a hand in fashioning the Hitler effigy. One lady provided the jacket, another the trousers and so on until the Fuehrer's rig-out was as accurate as possible. A dressmaker living in the road gave him the finishing touches. The Chief Fire Watcher in Hanover Road made the face, the boys fitted up the gallows from which he was hung and the adults laid the foundations of the bonfire. Then someone suggested that they burn Goering too, and soon the corpulent Reichsmarschall – complete with rows of Iron Crosses – was seated on a chair at Hitler's feet. Next to them was a battered doll, face and body darkened with red paint as a reminder of the misery the Nazis had brought to humanity. The bonfire was lit at 9.30pm, and almost immediately Hitler began to go up in flames. Amid cries of 'Don't let him end up so soon, let him linger', a hose was applied to the effigy in order to prolong the burning.

Dancing in the streets in Eindhoven, Holland.

WHEN THE LIGHTS GO ON AGAIN

In Coventry, the scene of a devastating air raid in November 1940, the day was marked by a Thanksgiving Service in the ruins of the city's medieval cathedral. The sky was grey with rain, but the precincts of the cathedral were bright with bunches of flowers brought by worshippers. There was also a large pewter bowl in which Coventry people who had lost relations were invited to place the names of 'dear ones'. A mile or two from the cathedral more earthy celebrations were taking place. Two days before VE Day a life-sized image of Hitler, stuffed with straw, had been suspended by the neck over the middle of a suburban street. As dusk approached on VE night, a self-styled 'Mayor and Wife' – both of them men – presided over the effigy's funeral. The 'Mayoress' was a local builder, the fattest and jolliest man in the street, and now squeezed into a frilly white dress and wearing a blonde wig made out of rope ends. The effigy was slowly let down and then borne off on a couple of planks to a common at the bottom of the road. In setting light to the bonfire the 'Mayoress' contrived to singe her elegant wig.

This, at least, was one of the minor mishaps of VE night. In Herefordshire, over-enthusiastic bonfire-building had succeeded in setting ablaze about four square miles of scrubland. Sunderland proved an even more dangerous place to celebrate VE Day. At teatime that afternoon someone loosed off a number of live 20mm Oerlikon shells from a ship lying at anchor in the Weare. Miraculously no one was hurt, although one old lady, dozing quietly by her radio in Osborne Street, Fulwell, was rudely woken as one of the shells embedded itself in the ceiling above her head. Not so lucky was the 8,000-ton Liberty Ship *Horace Binney*, which struck a German mine 36 miles off the coast of Holland. Though badly damaged, she remained afloat and was towed into an anchorage off the port of Deal.

In small towns and local communities the main organized events of the day centred around children. There were street parties, fancy dress parades and sports days. Many streets had been collecting money for weeks for their parties but rationing ensured that the catering arrangements were somewhat hit-and-miss. Many years after the war a Bristol housewife still shuddered at the recollection of a huge bowl of custard made with dried milk and saccharine. An Ipswich housewife struck a topical note at a fancy dress parade, equipping her small son as 'Rationing', in a suit made from old curtains covered with out-of-date coupons.

WHEN THE LIGHTS GO ON AGAIN

There was only one serious outbreak of violence on VE Day, in Halifax, Nova Scotia. Eight thousand sailors and merchant seamen went on an orgy of looting allegedly sparked off by the way they had been exploited by the town's tightfisted hoteliers and tradespeople. Downtown Halifax was reduced to a shambles. Inevitably, the liquor stores were the first to be rifled: 'At the height of the turbulence men and women reeled through the streets, carrying cases of beer ... whisky or rum ... or walked with hands full of bottles. The parks were turned into beer gardens as couples or groups sprawled on the grass with a case of whisky – an entire year's ration – beside them. It was a vicious celebration, the worst incident of the war in Halifax.' Before a curfew cleared the streets, two had died and over five million dollars' worth of damage had been done.

THE MORNING AFTER

VE+1 arrived leaving many people with a feeling of flatness and anti-climax. The outward trappings of war began to fall away, but the daily routine seemed little changed by the announcement of peace. A retired schoolmistress wrote in her diary: 'Today is a sort of anti-climax. It seemed strange to some extent that we could no longer say "There's a war on". The last of the blackout curtains were taken down – they were not conspicuous and I haven't drawn them this winter, when we weren't so particular as we used to be. A jar of anti-mustard-gas ointment was consigned to the dustbin. I wish we could be told what to do with our gas masks. I'm tired of seeing them hanging in the hall.' Some time after the war a London woman reflected: 'It was almost worse than during the war. First of all we had this tremendous feeling of elation. It's over. I remember standing outside Buckingham Palace with the cheering crowds seeing the King and Queen and Churchill. We had to walk the seven miles back to Roehampton. Bonfires on the way, and people dancing in the street. The elation lasted for a week or two and then there was a feeling of disillusion, the kind of thing that happens after a party. The morning after had come.'

On Thursday a Mass-Observer walking through Trafalgar Square noted that the decorations themselves now looked rather war-worn and weary. On a soap box a young Bevin Boy (could it have been one of the heroes of VE Night?) was talking nonsense to a crowd gathered round him. In another guise he might have been an agitator, but now he was just enjoying a brief spree of pure exhibitionism, encouraged by an audience who were still in a good-natured and playful mood.

For a rating serving on the battleship *Renown* the 'morning after' brought a surprise. Returning to his ship, stationed in the Firth of Forth, he found that a German admiral and his staff were on board. 'They were in the gunroom and had come to turn Norway and Norwegian waters over to us. With them they had a petty officer steward who had to live, screened off, in the pantry. Many of the ship's company came in to have a look at him, and he was so terrified that when having his supper, I'm told, he could not find his mouth and kept pushing his fork into the wrong part of his face.' The Germans' supper, the rating noted, consisted of Spam and cold potatoes followed by bread and butter and black treacle. Later, strolling along a companionway, he spotted one of the Germans. Making a dumb show, he pointed the way out to the deck. The reply came back in a perfect Oxford accent, 'It's all right, thank you, I was in this ship quite often in peacetime and know my way about.'

U776 surrendered and was sailed up the Thames by the Royal Navy, only to heel over on the mud at Westminster when the tide ran out.

'OUR DEAR CHANNEL ISLANDS'

In St Helier, the capital of Jersey, largest of the Channel Islands, another German admiral was preparing to take his leave of the war. Vice-Admiral Hüffmeier, affectionately known by his men as 'the Madman', was a hardline Nazi who had vowed to put up a last-ditch struggle. On 7 May orders were still going out from his headquarters to improve the coastal fortifications. These were discreetly ignored by his subordinates and the 36,000-strong garrison. That evening the inhabitants of St Helier could be glimpsed bringing out the Union Jacks which had stayed hidden away since the Germans had landed in June 1940. VE-1 was also marked by the issue of four ounces of dried peas to all the Islanders, along with an increase in the bread ration to 6lb a head. In another belated gesture of goodwill thirty people jailed for offences against German regulations were released.

The medal struck to commemorate the liberation of Jersey on 9 May.

WHEN THE LIGHTS GO ON AGAIN

In June 1942 the Germans had ordered the confiscation of all wireless sets in the Channel Islands. In Jersey a priest had died in German hands after a conviction for illicit wireless listening, and a cinema projectionist had been sent to Buchenwald after the discovery of wireless equipment in his projection room. Now, on the morning of VE Day, loudspeakers were erected in the Royal Square, St Helier, which by 3pm was packed with Islanders tensely waiting to hear Churchill's speech. One observer recalled, 'As the Town Church clock struck three a cheer went up at the announcement that Mr Churchill was to speak; his statement was punctuated by cheers, especially when he referred to "our dear Channel Islands" and when, at the conclusion, the Bailiff hoisted the Union Jack and Jersey flag over the courthouse … many wept unashamedly.'

The German surrender in the Channel Islands was a protracted affair. Two British destroyers, *Bulldog* and *Beagle*, had arrived off Guernsey at 2pm on VE Day. Aboard *Bulldog* was the chief British representative, Brigadier Snow. Snow's first visitor was a young German naval officer, Captain-Lieutenant Arnim Zimmermann, who pointed out to the British that as the armistice did not come into general effect for another 10 hours 'Your ships must move away immediately from these shores'. Zimmermann was informed that the only item on the agenda was immediate surrender. He departed to report to Hüffmeier while the two destroyers continued to steam up and down under the muzzles of the Madman's heavy shore batteries. Then, just after midnight, 'Out of the darkness came a German armed trawler … and, as we swept searchlights over the German vessel, there came into the rays a white eight-oared cutter. In her stern sat the same naval officer, but with him was a resplendent figure in light blue army greatcoat with great red lapels. He was Major-General Heine, of the German Army.' Just over seven hours later the Major-General was not looking quite so resplendent as, with shaking hand, he signed the surrender document on *Bulldog's* quarterdeck. At 7.45 the German trawler chugged back to St Peter Port, flying the White Ensign and carrying 20 men of the Royal Artillery to a rapturous welcome. Later that day Guernsey's chief citizen, the Bailiff, handed in at the post office the first telegram despatched to a British address since June 1940:

HIS MAJESTY THE KING, BUCKINGHAM PALACE, LONDON. AFTER NEARLY FIVE YEARS OF GERMAN OCCUPATION THE PEOPLE OF YOUR BAILIWICK OF GUERNSEY RESPECTFULLY BEG YOUR MAJESTY TO ACCEPT THEIR HUMBLE DUTY AND UNSHAKEN LOYALTY. VICTOR G. CAREY, LIEUTENANT-GOVERNOR AND BAILIFF.

Jersey was liberated by *Beagle* a few hours later. Two lieutenants and four ordinary seamen were the first men ashore, where delirious crowds carried them shoulder high to the office of the Harbour Master. On board *Beagle* the island's Lieutenant-Governor, Alexander Coutanche, was enjoying his first pink gin for years. An even greater luxury – after years of intense privation – was the bar of soap he found in the basin of the washroom. The paraphernalia of German occupation disappeared virtually overnight. Their troops were marched off to a camp outside St Helier and the hated scarlet-lettered *Verboten* notices were torn down and thrown into the harbour, where they slowly floated out to sea on the tide. Lights blazed late into the night and all over the Channel Islands hidden wirelesses, bicycles and even motor cars made their reappearance. Channel Islanders gazed, awestruck, at the groaning shelves of bread in the bakers' shops. On Saturday 12 May a convoy of 50 ships arrived off the Channel Islands bringing with them dimly remembered luxuries – flour, meat, biscuits, tea, chocolate, tobacco, soap, coal and house gas. Even the German POWs working on the quay in St Helier cheered lustily as the first landing craft nosed its way into the harbour. A small minority was excluded from these celebrations, the reviled 'Jerrybags', women who had taken German lovers during the occupation. Immediately after the liberation a number of them were the objects of private acts of revenge – no Channel Islander was ever accused of collaboration. Some of the 'Jerrybags' were beaten up, others had their heads shaved, a punishment also meted out to collaborators in France. At least one had to be rescued from an angry mob by British troops.

A Paris department store decorated in preparation for the Victory celebrations.

above VE Day in the Place de la Concorde.

left and opposite Mementoes of the French Victory celebrations: matchbooks honouring the *entente cordiale* and a calendar in which General de Gaulle occupies pride of place below Roosevelt, Stalin and Churchill.

French cartoonist Dubout's irreverent look at the way Parisians celebrated victory.

left Celebrations were still in full swing in Paris three days later.

SURRENDER IN BERLIN

Early on VE Day Air Chief-Marshal Tedder and the US Air Force General 'Tooey' Spaatz flew to Berlin to participate in the formal German surrender to the Russians. Along for the ride were a number of Eisenhower's personal staff. There was an interminable wait after their arrival in Berlin – somewhat eased by copious supplies of caviar, Rhine wine and cognac – before the party was summoned to Zhukov's headquarters in the Wehrmacht engineering college in a north-eastern suburb of Berlin. A remarkable sight greeted their eyes when they entered the surrender hall at about 11pm. Captain Butcher, Eisenhower's naval aide, recorded his impressions: 'The huge room was banked with klieg lights, blinding as we stepped in from the dim hallway. Everything seemed to be set up for the convenience of the Russian press, who numbered close to a hundred and swarmed around in shouting bedlam. Movie cameras were ready in almost every conceivable spot. Microphones sprouted from the floor, hung from the ceiling; they and the klieg lights created a veritable spider web of wires and cables.'

Zhukov arrived with Andrei Vyshinsky, the Soviet Deputy Commissar for Foreign Affairs, in close attendance. Butcher noted, 'I was surprised at the way a civilian ... hovered over the entire proceedings, deferred to even by Zhukov. Even in this moment of Soviet military victory, the Kremlin was stepping in to take charge.' Silence fell as Keitel, accompanied by Friedeburg and Colonel-General Stumpf (representing the Luftwaffe), made his appearance. Noticing the French General de Lattre de Tassigny, Keitel was heard to mutter, 'The French are here! That's all we need.' Then, recovering his icy demeanour, he jerked up his field marshal's baton in a salute and took his place at the table, eyeing the jostling journalists with contempt. As he signed the document the press kicked and fought to get a better view. Keitel's steely gaze bored through them as Friedeburg and Stumpf added their signatures. Then the three German officers rose as one and, with Prussian military precision, stalked from the room.

Now the celebrations began in earnest, and in true Russian style. An hour after the departure of the German High Command the surrender hall had become a banqueting hall, with an orchestra

Field Marshal Keitel preparing to sign the instrument of surrender at Zhukov's headquarters in Berlin on 8 May. On his right is General Weidling, on his left Admiral Friedeburg.

installed on the balcony. The eating, and toasting, went on for four hours. Several Russians slid under the table into comradely oblivion. Eisenhower's secretary contrived to remain sober by drinking water rather than vodka: 'As the party broke up just before dawn [we women] agreed there had been between 24 and 29 individual toasts, each requiring five to ten minutes for translation, plus the musical chord, and the final, deadly bottoms-up.' The official interpreter had gallantly kept abreast of the toasts for most of the banquet, but towards the end even he could no longer make any sense of them. In a final display of characteristically erratic Russian hospitality, the visiting party were taken on a dawn tour of the ruins of Berlin, a sight calculated to sober up even the most inebriated member of the delegation from Rheims. They took off from Tempelhof airport at seven in the morning.

MOSCOW

As they flew westwards, immense crowds were already gathering in Moscow's Red Square to celerate their own VE Day. The shadows of the Cold War would soon close in, but on VE Day in Moscow 'it was

left A *laisser-passer* for the Victory parade in Moscow's Red Square which took place in June.

opposite The British Victory parade in Bremerhaven on 12 May. For the majority of British troops serving in northern Europe, VE Day itself passed almost unnoticed. Nevertheless, there was a small surprise at dinner – a free pint of beer for each man. Less agreeable was the determination, now that the war was over, of spit-and-polish minded NCOs to return to the endless bull of peacetime soldiering. A member of the King's Shropshire Light Infantry wrote, 'Sparks began to fly – not in the form of .88 shells ... but in the form of Blanco, drill, PT and last but certainly not least DPs (Drill Parades) turning ... mud begrimed battle veterans into a company of smart, clean-shaven and well-behaved men.'

sufficient to look like a foreigner to be kissed, hugged and generally feted'. The famous 'Red' Dean of Canterbury, Dr Hewlett Johnson, who was on a goodwill tour of Russia on behalf of the Anglo-Soviet Medical Fund, watched amazed as 'A dense crowd, enthusiastic and genial, released at last from the long strain of war, blocked our road and engulfed us, cheering every Englishman or American. They seized General Younger, a British officer in full uniform, and tossing him in the air, caught him as gently as if he were a babe. My turn came next.'

The Times' Moscow correspondent watched the spectacle from a roof top: 'Hundreds of thousands of people since early morning have been streaming into the centre of Moscow. The crowds fill the broad street, two or three times the width of Whitehall, that runs below the western walls of the Kremlin past the university and the Lenin Library to the Moskva River. They line the river bank below the terrace. They are packing the Red Square ... Crowds sweep each side of St Basil's Church towards the bridge over the Moskva River, away towards the theatre square, where a bandstand has been erected for street dancing, and into the dark streets of Chinatown. Wireless sets are broadcasting Tipperary, sung by a Red Army choir. It is a homely democratic crowd, in which generals and soldiers, commissars and workers, mingle.'

That afternoon Dr Hewlett Johnson went with the Patriarch of the Russian Orthodox Church to St Basil's. Approaching the entrance, they pushed their way through 'crowds such as I have seldom seen before. Russian churches are chairless. People stand, and on that day so tight was the wedge of humanity that movement was well-nigh impossible. At length we reached the enclosure which shuts the altar off from the congregation and were given a place of honour between screen and people. Near us sang the choir, men and women in everyday dress; the Cantor led the service with an immense voice which carried far down the huge building and boomed out to the crowds in the street.'

The sheer scale of the Moscow celebrations dwarfed those in other Euorpean capitals. The victory salute was fired by 1,000 guns, lined up wheel to wheel on the Moskva embankment and each one firing thirty salvoes. That night, after Stalin's broadcast to the Russian people, there was a spectacular firework display, and the sky was swept by the beams of hundreds of coloured searchlights. Looking up, Dr Hewlett Johnson watched them playing on 'a gigantic red banner held by invisible cables from invisible balloons'.

PRAGUE IS FREED

On 9 May there remained only one pocket of German resistance, in Slovakia. The Czechoslovak National Army had planned a rising for 7 May but they were pre-empted on 4 May by the citizens of Prague who, excited by news of the American advance into Bohemia, took to the streets. The next day the National Army rose in open revolt against Field Marshal Schörner's Army Group Centre. Even in the dying stages of the war the Waffen SS moved with its customary ferocity. As their tank columns closed in on Prague – a city which had survived unscathed through five years of war – the radio station 'Prague Czechoslovakia', broadcasting in English and Russian, made an appeal for air support to hold off the German armour. On 6 May the calls became increasingly desperate – 'Send your tanks, send your

One of the first Russian tanks to enter Prague on 9 May. The Russian occupation of the city brought an end to the final pocket of German resistance of the war.

Two small citizens of Brussels wearing their Allies' colours on VE Day.

tanks and aircraft, help us save Prague.' The Americans held back. On 7 May three US Army vehicles had reached the western outskirts of Prague, but Eisenhower had already been told by Truman that he was unwilling to risk American lives for political purposes. The Americans in Prague were ordered to drive back 50 miles to General Patton's 3rd Army on the Pilsen Line.

For the next 36 hours murderous confusion reigned. Heavy street fighting raged in Prague. To the east, German units falling back from the Russians left behind them a trail of destruction. The small town of Konetopy, 22 miles north-east of Prague, was burned to the ground and its inhabitants mown down by firing squads. Vlasov's Army – a force of Soviet renegades who had fought on the German side – arrived on the scene and threatened to turn on their masters. To the west, German formations were racing Russian spearheads to the safety of the American lines. It was left to Marshal Konev to finish the matter. At 8pm on 8 May he transmitted details of the German capitulation to all their units in western Czechoslovakia. The German commanders there were given three hours in which to reply. When no reply came Konev ordered a massive artillery barrage and, as it lifted, the 12 armies on his front resumed their westward progress. In the small hours of 9 May armoured units of General Lelyushenko's 4th Guards Army reached the outer suburbs of Prague. At the same time the SS garrison in the city were streaming westward in an attempt to escape the jaws of the Red Army encirclement closing around them. Later in the day Soviet tanks pushed on into the ancient city, their tracks rolling over a carpet of lilacs thrown in their path by its overjoyed population. In the city whose annexation had started the inexorable slide to war, the European struggle against Nazism had come to an end.

Wearing the national dress of Normandy, the 'children of the beaches' remember D-Day at Arromanches in June 1945.

An American poster protesting about German presence in Czechoslovakia.

Charles Cundall's painting of the Service of Thanksgiving, attended by the Royal Family and the Prime Minister, on Sunday 13 May at St Paul's Cathedral.

Part Three
AFTERMATH

Three among millions of displaced persons: Mrs Eva Bass with her baby and son go through the gate to their new home at Fort Ontario, N.Y. Formerly a nightclub singer in Paris, Mrs Bass was a prisoner of the Nazis during the war.

EUROPE IN RUINS

An inventory of Europe in May 1945 would have made grim reading. The continent had been prostrated by war. Cities such as Dresden and Warsaw had been razed to the ground. By April 1945 almost 90 per cent of Warsaw's buildings had been destroyed by the retreating Germans, and more than half its population of 1.3 million killed, the equivalent of the combined British and American military losses on all fronts throughout the war. Over a million died in the siege of Leningrad. Along with great cities small communities were pounded to dust by aerial bombardment, massed artillery and street battles. The small town of Wiener Neustadt, near Vienna, was left with only 18 houses standing and a population reduced from 45,000 to 860. In the war and its immediate aftermath some 60 million civilians – about 10 per cent of Europe's population – were uprooted from their homes.

The Soviet Union had emerged as immeasurably the strongest power in Europe, but by the war's end it was a crippled giant. The economy was in ruins. Despite the prodigious Russian output of war materials, she had lost some 30,000 factories during the conflict. About a quarter of all the Soviet Union's property had been destroyed. Over 2,000 towns and 70,000 villages remained, for the moment, as

A year after the war, the great black bulk of Cologne Cathedral rises above a city barely returning to normal. Over 60 per cent of Cologne's residential buildings were destroyed by Allied bombing.

little more than map references. Twenty-five million of her people were homeless.

In the Soviet Union approximately 7.7 million civilians died on both sides of the line. Russian military losses amounted to 13.6 million of whom 2.6 million died in unspeakable conditions in German captivity. In all, about eight million Poles died as a result of the war, most of them under German occupation in their own country. In the final count, German civilian and military losses were about equally divided:3.25 million servicemen and 3.8 million non-combatants. Over six million died in the concentration and extermination camps.

Huge tracts of land had been devastated by flooding and scorched earth tactics. Crippling shortages of labour, machinery, fertilizer seed and livestock combined with a severe drought to produce a disastrous grain harvest, almost 50 per cent lower than the pre-war average outside the Soviet Union. In Britain bread rationing was introduced, a measure never contemplated during the war. A journalist visiting Paris observed, 'You don't throw apple cores into the waste basket. You fling them out of the window – to be eaten.'

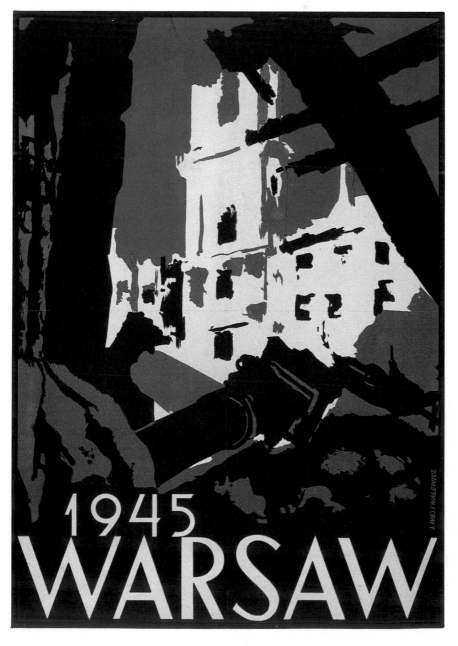

A poster evoking the tragedy of Warsaw, half of whose population had died, and 90 per cent of whose buildings had been destroyed, by April 1945.

THE PUNISHMENT OF COLLABORATORS

To hunger were added the deep, festering wounds left by occupation and collaboration. In France the purge of collaborators – known as *l'épuration* – lasted from September 1944 to the end of 1949. Just over 2,000 death sentences were handed down, of which 768 were carried out. All death sentences on women and minors were automatically commuted by President de Gaulle. At least a dozen times as many collaborators were summarily executed in the period immediately after liberation. The entertainer Maurice Chevalier, whose only crime had been to entertain French prisoners of war in Germany, escaped from the firing squad only by the skin of his teeth.

On 23 July 1945 Marshal Pétain was arraigned on a charge of treason. Alone of the Vichy survivors he had requested to be allowed to return to France to face trial: 'At my age, there is only one thing one still fears. That is not to have done all one's duty, and I wish to do mine.' In court Pétain wore the simplest uniform of a Marshal of France and the Médaille Militaire, the only decoration shared by simple soldiers and great commanders. When his lawyer begged him to take his Marshal's baton into the court, Pétain replied scornfully, 'That would be theatrical.' In his last words to the court before sentence Pétain said, 'My thought, my only thought, was to remain with them [the French] on the soil of France, according to my promise, so as to protect them and to lessen their sufferings.' The court remained unmoved. On 15 August the ninety-year-old Marshal was sentenced to death. President de Gaulle commuted the sentence to one of life imprisonment and the old man was confined on the Ile de Yeu off the Vendée coast. In June 1951, enfeebled and no longer lucid, he was freed. He was dead within a month, passing away within two days of the ex-Crown Prince Rupprecht of Bavaria, his old adversary at Verdun.

below Marshal Pétain listens impassively to proceedings at his trial on a charge of treason in August 1945.

below right Pierre Laval's trial followed soon after Pétain's. To the end he declared himself a French patriot.

above Belgian collaborators rounded up and temporarily imprisoned in a cage in Antwerp zoo.

A young Dane accused of collaboration is paraded through the streets of Copenhagen shortly after the city's liberation.

Pierre Laval, the Vichy Prime Minister, stood trial two months after Pétain. The proceedings were frequently interrupted as execrations were hurled down on him from the public gallery. On 14 October, four days after being sentenced to death, he took poison. He was found to be still alive and throughout the following day doctors laboured to revive him for his appointment with the firing squad.

In north-west Europe Danish intelligence agents posted on the Jutland-German border plucked hundreds of collaborators, suspected traitors, German Gestapo agents and SS officials from the columns of retreating Germans and wandering refugees. Six weeks after the liberation more than 1,100 arrests were made at the border and the number of those arrested within Denmark totalled 20,000, among them hundreds of 'field mattresses' – young women who had gone with German soldiers. As in France there were a great many summary executions by the Resistance. It was a sign of the prevailing bitterness in Denmark – the Third Reich's 'showcase' province – that the death penalty, whose introduction had been successfully resisted during the occupation, was restored for the worst cases of collaboration.

Of all the occupied countries of western Europe, Norway pursued its collaborators with the most vigour. In France 94 out of every 100,000 citizens had been imprisoned for collaboration; in Norway 633 out of every 100,000 were punished, including the 81-year-old Knut Hamsun, Norway's greatest living writer. The leader of the Norwegian Nazi Party, Vidkun Quisling, underwent a protracted trial during which he was subjected to a 'severe' physical and psychological examination which included 'electrical' probing of his brain. This did not prevent him from delivering a final defence speech, without notes, which lasted almost eight hours, after which he was sentenced to death.

Two young Frenchmen who confessed to having been trained as spies and saboteurs in Germany, after being sentenced to life imprisonment with hard labour. Collaborators with German military service charged with minor offences were offered active service in Indo-China as an alternative to imprisonment.

With head shaven and surrounded by a jeering crowd, a young Frenchwoman is punished for taking a German lover by being driven out of her home town.

AFTERMATH

Ironically, collaborators accused of relatively minor crimes sometimes received far harsher treatment than those who had committed more serious offences. The minor offenders were the first to be tried after the liberation, when feelings still ran very high. In Holland 35 special courts, each consisting of five judges, were set up to deal with the major cases of collaboration, while a host of smaller tribunals were left to try the small fry. By the autumn of 1945 some 96,000 Dutch collaborators remained behind bars and the tribunals' backlog had swollen so alarmingly that a system of 'out of court' settlements was introduced. If the accused did not agree to the proposed 'settlement', then he would stand trial. About 80 per cent gratefully accepted settlement.

GERMANY'S MISERY

In the middle of this sea of misery and destruction lay Germany. The great power of 1939 had ceased to exist. Savage fighting had raged across her territory. Waves of refugees had washed across Germany, at first fleeing east away from the bombing and then cascading west away from the Russians. Bombing had gouged the heart out of her towns, cities and industries. For every ton of bombs dropped on Britain 315 had descended on Germany. Mervyn Peake, despatched to Germany as a war artist, wrote home to his wife about the cities through which he had passed: 'They are no more. They are relics. Terrible as the bombing of London was, it is as absolutely nothing – nothing – compared with this unutterable desolation. Imagine

Oscar Nerlinger's depiction of the war against famine in postwar Germany.

Chelsea in fragments with not a single house with any more than a few weird-shaped walls where it once stood, and you will get an idea in miniature of what Mannheim and Wiesbaden are like – yet these are only two of the towns we have seen....'

The surreal charades of the Fuehrerbunker were now transferred to the less apocalyptic setting of Flensburg where, until 22 May, the Doenitz government exercised a phantom authority. Its initiatives included the establishment of an 'information service' consisting of an old radio set housed in a school classroom. The Minister of Food's sole function was to provide the desultory meetings with a constant supply of whisky. The popular entertainer, wit and author, Arthur Marshall – then a colonel in Army intelligence – has recalled the

After being rounded up in Flensburg, the members of Doenitz's government were herded into a courtyard at gunpoint where they faced a 'firing squad' of photographers and newsreel men. Seen here are Speer, Doenitz and Jodl.

A shattered German .88 points skyward in front of the Reichstag ruins, which were defended to the last by a large German garrison of about 5000 men, over half of whom were killed.

bizarre atmosphere which hung over Flensburg. Every day he found himself exchanging punctilious salutes with Field Marshal Keitel, soon to stand trial at Nuremberg. Lunching one day on the *Patria*, the liner moored by the quay at Flensburg, Marshall watched an officer of the Kriegsmarine instructing a group of young naval officers in U-boat tactics. Presiding over the scene was a huge bronze bust of Hitler. Shortly afterwards a gang of workmen arrived and sawed off his head.

The Doenitz government was put out of its agony at the end of May, but for the people of Berlin the agony was only just beginning. The American General Lucius D. Clay described Germany's capital as a 'city of the dead'. At least 150,000 civilians died in the final battle for Berlin. Twenty years later bodies were still being unearthed on building sites, in ruins and private gardens, and in parks where they had been hastily shovelled into mass graves. On a snowy day in the winter of 1972 workers constructing an exhibition park on the site of Berlin's old Lehrter station uncovered two skeletons in an unmarked grave. One was that of a tall man, the other short and burly. Lodged in their jawbones were splinters from glass cyanide ampoules. Subsequently the remains were identified as those of Ludwig Stumpfegger, Hitler's surgeon, and Martin Bormann.

Among the first British soldiers to enter Berlin was a Colonel Byford-Jones, who had known the city well before the war: 'The Unter Den Linden, now embankments of burnt-out buildings that were once stately palaces, the pavements littered with wreckage. Between these embankments, where the proud Wehrmacht had marched, were hundreds of ex-Wehrmacht prisoners, unshaven ... filthy, tattered, empty food tins tied to the string that girt their waists, their eyes empty. Like an army of zombies, they moved silently, their feet bound in sacking, as if propelled by some external power ... Rising in the heat of the day came a hideous smell of dampness, of charred remains, of thousands of putrefying bodies.'

To Tom Pocock, who toured the Russian sector in July, the ruins of Berlin 'seemed eternal: dunes of rubble stretching away amongst tottering walls of tall buildings eviscerated by fire. Main roads had been cleared, their sides embanked with rough walls of broken bricks beyond which rose steep screes of broken masonry, pitted cliffs of ornate façades and, here and there, bared steel girders like warped climbing frames in a children's playground.' Long, silent lines of women sorted the rubble by hand – there were no implements. 'Sometimes we passed other lines of women carrying buckets, waiting outside the less-ruined buildings, where the Allied troops had already been billeted, in the hope of being given a swill of left-overs after the soldiers had eaten.'

In 1945 the great majority of Berliners were struggling to survive on about 800 calories a day. In March 1946 the ration in the British sector dropped in some instances to a mere 400 calories a day, less than that given to the inmates of Bergen-Belsen. In the summer of 1945 the number of mouths to feed increased daily by about 20,000 as German refugees, ejected from the east by the Russians, streamed into the Berlin zone of occupation. In a grim reversal of fortune many of them were crammed into cattle trucks for the journey, where they became the helpless prey of marauding groups of bandits. Those who reached Berlin found little help. Under the shattered roof of the Stettin station the British journalist Norman Clark saw 'scores of people, all ravenous and starving, for whom nothing could be done until death'.

Immediately after the war medical supplies were virtually

Berliners protest about bread shortages.

A German woman picks through a refuse dump outside Heidelberg in search of food.

non-existent. In the British sector 43 of the 44 hospitals had been destroyed or badly damaged. Burst water mains and ruptured sewers spread typhoid. Mosquitoes fed on the corpses rotting in the rubble and then spread dysentery, which in July killed six out of every ten babies born in Berlin. The crumbling ruins also harboured a deadlier peril than disease. The city was lethal with unexploded ammunition – shells, mines and grenades – of which about 1,500 tons were recovered daily.

THE POTSDAM CONFERENCE

It was in Potsdam, in the southern suburbs of Berlin, that Truman, Stalin and Churchill gathered for the last great conference of the war, appropriately codenamed 'Terminal'. The Potsdam conference put the seal on the proposals for the future of central and eastern Europe which had been canvassed by the 'Big Three' at Teheran in November 1943 and agreed at Yalta in February 1945. The process resembled the formal carve-up of Africa by the colonial powers in the 19th century.

Churchill's personal physician, Lord Moran, recorded the atmosphere of brooding menace which hung over the place: 'The PM had called for a glass of whisky. Then we sat in silence for a long time looking at the lawn that sloped to a lake, into which, so it was said, the Russians had thrown some German soldiers who could not walk because of their wounds. Beyond the lake a field rose sharply to a wood. The only sign of life we could see was a Russian sentry who came out of the wood, looked round and disappeared into the trees. When the light had gone, a rifle shot, that seemed to come from the wood, broke the silence that had fallen on everything.'

Churchill had arrived in Berlin in a gloomy frame of mind, fretting over the outcome of the British general election, the result of which was to be declared on 26 July. Before leaving for Potsdam he had told Lord Moran, 'I dreamed that life was over. I saw – it was very vivid – my dead body under a white sheet on a table in an empty room. I recognized my bare feet projecting from under the sheet. It was very lifelike ... Perhaps this is the end.'

left and opposite The two conferences which determined the shape of the postwar world. Churchill, Roosevelt and Stalin at Yalta in February 1945; Churchill and Truman at Potsdam in the following July.

above Three years after the end of the war Berlin women still shouldered much of the work of reconstruction. In the autumn of 1945 Colonel Byford-Jones wrote: 'You could sense the absence of men wherever you went. Everywhere there were women alone, in pairs or groups, paying for their own drinks in cafés, cutting wood, moving debris, doing men's work. As the winter wore on every third woman or girl came out dressed in the trousers of her absent husband, brother or son.' In Berlin it was estimated that women outnumbered men by at least three to one.

AFTERMATH

The Prime Minister seemed unusually subdued on a tour of Berlin before the opening of the conference. He was taken to inspect Hitler's bunker and descended to Eva Braun's room, where a vase still contained the dried-up remains of a sprig of flowers placed there just before the end. Recovering his breath on a chair in the Chancellery garden, Churchill mopped his brow and observed that Hitler must have come up there to get some air and heard the Russian guns getting closer and closer. Later that day Moran attempted to raise Churchill's spirits by showing him a souvenir Iron Cross he had scooped up from the floor of the wrecked Chancellery building. But Churchill's only response was 'poor devils'. Then he spoke of what was dominating his mind: 'I shall be glad when this election business is over. It hovers over me like a vulture of uncertainty in the sky...'

Something far bigger also preoccupied Churchill, and before the conference was over he unburdened himself to Moran. On 23 July Churchill told him, 'I am going to tell you something that you must not tell any human being. We have split the atom. The report of the great experiment has just come in. A bomb was let off in some wild spot in New Mexico. It was only a 13lb bomb, but it made a crater half a mile across.' Moran's reply was, 'It is H.G. Wells stuff. It is the second coming.' Churchill went on, 'The secret has been wrested from nature... It gives the Americans the power to mould the world. If the Russians had got it, it would mean the end of civilization. It is to be used in Japan, on cities, not armies.'

Stalin was told about the atom bomb on the following day. His face betrayed no sign of surprise. Churchill wondered whether he had in fact understood Truman's casual, almost enigmatic, reference to the successful test. Perhaps he already knew that, in the fullness of time, the Soviet Union would have its own nuclear weapons.

When Churchill met Stalin in Moscow in October 1944, they sat down to discuss their respective postwar 'spheres of influence'. In his own *History of the Second World War*, Churchill recorded the discussion. On a piece of paper he scrawled the suggestion that the Russians should have 90 per cent influence in Rumania – for a trade-off of 10 per cent influence in Greece – 75 per cent in Bulgaria and 50 per cent in Yugoslavia and Hungary, the remaining percentages to be controlled by Britain. 'I pushed this across to Stalin ... Then he took his blue pencil and made a large tick upon it, and passed it back to us ... At length I said: "Might it not be thought rather cynical if it seemed we had disposed of these issues ... in such an offhand manner? Let us burn the paper." "No, you keep it," said Stalin.'

With this agreement under his belt, Churchill was able in the following December to instruct General Scobie, commander of British forces in Greece, to crush the power of the Communist-controlled partisan movement ELAM-ELAS, which controlled 90 per cent of the country. Stalin kept his side of the bargain, and on 19 February Churchill reported to the British cabinet, 'As regards Greece the Russian attitude could not have been more satisfactory. There was no suggestion on Premier Stalin's part of criticism of our policy ... The Prime Minister added that Premier Stalin had most scrupulously respected his acceptance of our position in Greece. He understood that the emissary sent to the USSR by the Greek Communists had first been put under house arrest, and then sent back. There had been no shadow of criticism in the Russian press at any time, and the conduct of the Russians in this matter had strengthened his view that when they made a bargain, they desired to keep it.'

above Churchill and Eden
set out on their tour of Berlin
before the start of the
Potsdam conference.

Churchill emerges from
Hitler's bunker in the
Chancellery grounds.

AFTERMATH

Over Poland, however, Stalin had absolutely no intention of keeping his side of the bargain. Poland's postwar frontiers had been mapped out in rough and ready fashion at Teheran. Stalin secured a western frontier with Poland which ran along the so-called 'Curzon Line', the border he had negotiated with Ribbentrop in 1939. Poland was to be compensated for this loss of territory by receiving 44,000 square miles of eastern Germany to the east of the Oder and Neisse rivers. In the process several million Poles and Germans would have to migrate westwards, a consequence about which the Poles were not consulted. To the 'Big Three', poring over a map of eastern Europe, this seemed merely one detail in the big picture. On 30 March 1939 Neville Chamberlain had written out, in his own hand a guarantee against aggression to Poland which Colonel Joseph Beck, the Polish Foreign Minister, had accepted 'between two flicks of the ash off his cigarette'. Now, in equally casual fashion, her postwar fate was decided. As a Foreign Office minute of the meeting between Churchill, Roosevelt, Stalin, Eden, Molotov and officials at the Soviet Embassy in Teheran on 1 December 1943 records: 'At this point Mr Molotov produced the Russian version of the Curzon line and a text of a wireless telegram from Lord Curzon giving all the place names. The Prime Minister asked whether Mr Molotov would object to the Poles getting the Oppeln district. Mr Molotov replied that he did not foresee any objection. The Prime Minister said that the Poles would be wise to take our advice. They were getting a country 300 miles square and that he was not prepared to make a great squawk about Lvov, and (turning to Marshal Stalin) he added that he did not think we were very far off in principle. President Roosevelt asked Marshal Stalin whether he thought a transfer of the population on a voluntary basis would be possible. Marshal Stalin said that it probably would be. Here the discussion about Poland came to an end.'

The political structure of postwar Poland was more problematic. Britain had gone to war over Poland's sovereignty and both Churchill and Roosevelt had initially hoped that, in the postwar period, the finalization of Poland's new frontiers would be followed by the establishment of a democratically elected government. It was left to the Germans to shatter their cosy illusion. In April 1943 they announced that in Katyn Wood they had discovered the bodies of 10,000 murdered Polish officers. The Polish government-in-exile in London called for a Red Cross inquiry into the massacre. The Soviet Union immediately broke off relations with them and set up their own Provisional Government of the Republic of Poland in Moscow. In 1944 it was moved to Lublin and in 1945 it was installed in Warsaw. The Poles in London were left out in the cold.

At Yalta Churchill managed to convince himself that Stalin had agreed to free elections in Poland after the war. He told the British cabinet, 'So far as Premier Stalin was concerned he [Churchill] was quite sure that he [Stalin] meant well to the world and to Poland. He [Churchill] did not himself think that there would be any resentment on the part of Russia about the agreement that had been made for free and fair elections in that country.' For Stalin this was merely an irrelevance. He was determined to close the gateway which had been the traditional invasion route from the West. Henceforward the government in Warsaw was to be 'a friend of the USSR'.

Only one eastern European country held back from a one-sided friendship with the Soviet Union. In Yugoslavia Stalin failed to secure his '50 per cent' sphere of influence. Yugoslavia was geographically the furthest Communist state from Moscow. She had

Chetniks (Yugoslav partisans loyal to General Mihailovic) hand in their arms near Palmonova on 9 May. Despite the smiles and Allied flags, they faced an uncertain future in Tito's Yugoslavia.

lost 1.5 million of her population during the occupation by the Italians and Germans, but had driven out the Axis forces single-handed, without a Red Army soldier setting foot on her soil. At the end of the war there were 800,000 armed partisans in Yugoslavia under the leadership of Marshal Tito. Throughout the war Stalin had supported Tito's rival, the royalist guerrilla leader General Draga Mihailovic. After some dithering the British had put their weight behind Tito, who was fighting the Germans while Mihailovic was not. When Fitzroy Maclean, the British representative with Tito, warned Churchill that he was a Communist, Churchill replied, 'Are you going to live in Yugoslavia after the war? No? Neither am I.' Communist or not, the Yugoslavs saw no reason to exchange German occupation for Russian domination. This independence was eventually to lead to Yugoslavia's expulsion from the Cominform, the successor organization to the Comintern, which Stalin had disbanded in 1943 as a gesture to his allies.

AFTERMATH
THE DISMEMBERMENT OF GERMANY

As far back as December 1941, while artillery was firing only 15 miles from the Kremlin in the suburbs of Moscow, Stalin had told Anthony Eden of Russia's postwar territorial demands. By 1943 the British were preparing plans of their own for the occupation of Germany and its dismemberment between the Allies. A cabinet committee under the chairmanship of Deputy Prime Minister Clement Attlee was established to prepare a report recommending a three-way division of Germany and a joint occupation of Berlin. Later these proposals were developed into a plan, codenamed Rankin C, which was drawn up by Lieutenant-General Morgan in his role as COSSAC (Chief of Staff to the Supreme Allied Commander, designate). At this stage in the war the only people not to be looking into the future were the Americans.

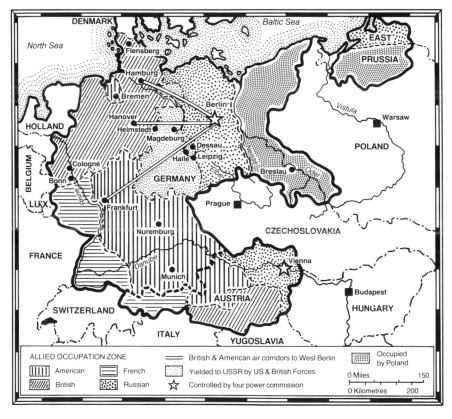

ALLIED OCCUPATION ZONE
American
British
French
Russian
British & American air corridors to West Berlin
Yielded to USSR by US & British Forces
Controlled by four power commission
Occupied by Poland
0 Miles 150
0 Kilometres 200

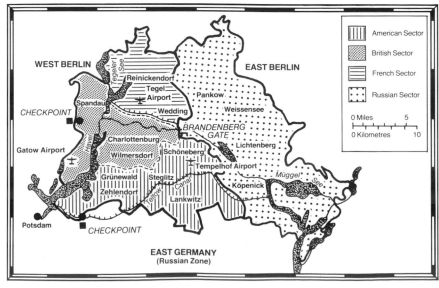

American Sector
British Sector
French Sector
Russian Sector
0 Miles 5
0 Kilometres 10

How the Allies divided Germany and Berlin under Four-Power control.

In the winter of 1943 a tripartite body, the European Advisory Committee (EAC) was set up to formulate a joint Allied policy for the postwar control and occupation of Germany. On 18 February 1944, at only its second formal meeting, the Russian EAC negotiator Gusev accepted the zonal proposals submitted by the British representative Sir William Strang. These were broadly based on the formula devised for Rankin C. They gave the Soviets almost 40 per cent of Germany's area, 36 per cent of its population and 33 per cent of its productive resources. Berlin, which lay within the Soviet zone and 100 miles from the Anglo-American demarcation line, was to be divided between the Allies. The British zone was in the north-west, the American in the south. The agreement between the Russians and the British presented the Americans with a fait accompli. Roosevelt had already made it clear that he desired a larger occupation zone for the US, in the north-west and stretching all the way to Stettin on the Oder. But the north-south relationship between the British and the Americans had been irreversibly decided many months before the invasion of Europe by a relatively low-level quartering decision. The American bases and depots in England had been located in the south and south-west, the British in the north and south-east. As Lieutenant-General Morgan later recalled, 'I do not believe that anyone at the time could have realized the full and ultimate implications of the quartering decision – which in all probability was made by some minor official in the War Office. But from it flowed all the rest.' The concentration of British and American troops, supplies and communications thus remained separate – the British on the left, in the north, and the Americans on the right, heading south, from Overlord to the final campaigns in the heart of Germany.

Berliners watch a British Military Policeman accompanied by a Berlin policeman.

AFTERMATH

At Yalta agreement was finally reached between the Allies on the dismemberment of Germany. On 11 February the Big Three formally accepted the respective zones which had been initially outlined in Rankin C. In addition France received a smaller occupation zone of her own, contiguous with her own borders and carved out of the British and American areas. Berlin, in the middle of the Soviet sector, was divided into four zones and was to be the headquarters of the Allied Control Council. Austria was split up in similar fashion, with Vienna providing a headquarters for a four-power commission. Five months later, on 5 June, Zhukov, Eisenhower, Montgomery and de Lattre de Tassigny signed the Declaration of Assumption of Supreme Authority in Germany, which spelled out the intentions of the conquerors and the obligations of the conquered. The Potsdam conference saw the formulation of the detailed political and economic principles which were to govern Germany during the control period.

The problems facing the Control Council defied immediate solution. An impressive array of orders was drawn up for the decentralization of the Germany economy, the destruction of German military potential, the exclusion of Nazis from public life and the trial of war criminals. Putting them into effect was another matter, as the Allies were rapidly forced to deal with a quite different set of problems – among them the restoration of communications and basic services, the provision of housing, the influx of huge numbers of refugees, and the activities of the black market. The French, who had been excluded from Potsdam, imposed a veto on sharing the resources of their own zone. (The French took their occupation duties extremely seriously; in Baden Baden, their headquarters town, the 7,600 French troops there outnumbered the German population.) The Russians went their own way. In one respect, at least, they put into

The badge worn by members of the quadripartite international patrol in Vienna.

Zhukov and Montgomery take the salute at a Victory march-past in Berlin.

effect the far-reaching reforms which were implicit in the economic policy formulated at Potsdam. In the autumn of 1945 seven million acres of land were confiscated and redistributed. The Soviets were equally thorough about reparations. During the course of 1944 they had extracted almost 2,000 million dollars' worth of resources from Rumania. Before the guns fell silent in Berlin they were already dismantling the industrial plant which remained intact in eastern Germany and shipping it eastwards. In the prevailing economic chaos of the Soviet Union most of it rusted away in remote railway sidings.

AFTERMATH
THE BLACK MARKET

The immediate problem for most Germans in the occupied zones was simply one of survival. The instrument of survival was the black market, an alternative underground economy whose powerful gravitational pull sucked both occupiers and occupied into its orbit. In the black market the basic unit of exchange was the cigarette. Five cigarettes could buy you sex. Twenty-five cartons of cigarettes – costing about $20 at an American PX – could be used by an entrepreneurially-minded GI to purchase a Leica camera. Back in the United States the camera could be sold for $600. With the $600, 750 cartons of cigarettes could be bought and traded for 30 Leicas worth $18,000. In this fashion fortunes could be made.

The Germans coined a word, *Kippensammler*, for a collector of cigarette ends. Seven butts could be recycled into one cigarette, and with one cigarette you could enter the complicated world in which Persian rug might be exchanged for 100lb of potatoes or a fur coat for a box of Spam or C-Rations. A British private, William Peters, observed the black market in operation in Cologne: 'Around the cathedral there is the usual black market. Sight-seeing Americans are besieged for anything – cigarettes, candies and food. People offer all sorts of objects for sale. An old man followed me and offered me an outdoor thermometer. He wanted some cigarettes in exchange. I gave him one and told him to keep the thermometer.'

This clandestine economic activity seemed to keep the entire population on the move. A visitor from Switzerland reported: 'Day after day, night after night, the people crowd on to the railway platform by the hundreds, many with small children, all with suitcases and rucksacks on their backs. They have heard that

A 19-year-old *Kippensammler* (cigarette-end-collector) on the streets of Berlin. Cigarettes were the staple currency of the city and one packet might change hands over a dozen times, bringing to a succession of people the basic goods on which their lives or health depended.

somewhere – perhaps 100 kilometres, perhaps 300 kilometres away – there is a village where potatoes or flour or a bit of pork fat can be got on the black market. So there they are going. If the trains run at all, they run two to ten hours late. They are unlit and, because of the coal shortage, unheated. The people are squashed into the carriages like sardines into a tin. Such is life in Germany today. The German goes hungry. He freezes. He sees his children die. He has become like a helpless, hunted animal.' The trains which carried Germans on these expeditions rapidly acquired nicknames. The 'Nicotine Line' took its passengers to the tobacco fields near Pfalz. The interzonal train from Osnabruck, near the North Sea, to Berlin was known as the 'Fish Express'; on the return journey it became the 'Silk Stocking Express'.

The rigid monetary controls imposed by the British and American authorities served only to encourage the black market. To this was added a flood of Reichsmarks from the Russians, who had been provided with the plates to print the currency by the Americans. Many

Daily black market bartering in a Berlin park, whose trees still bear the marks of war.

of the Red Army soldiers had not been paid for months, in some cases years. The Russians made up for this with a completely uncontrolled printing of Reichsmarks. His pockets bulging with the new currency, 'Ivan' was able to exchange the equivalent of $300 for a fountain pen or up to $1,000 for a Mickey Mouse watch.

Currency tokens issued by the Allied occupying powers.

THE PROCESS OF DENAZIFICATION

For many Germans the most prized black market item was the so-called 'Persil Certificate', a document which officially cleared the bearer of any complicity in Nazism. At Nuremberg in November, 21 of Hitler's intimate collaborators went on trial. William L. Shirer watched them in the dock: 'Goering, eighty pounds lighter than when last I saw him, in a faded Luftwaffe uniform without insignia and obviously pleased that he had been given the Number One place in the dock – a sort of belated recognition of his place in the Nazi hierarchy ... Rudolf Hess ... his face emaciated, his deep-set eyes staring vacantly into space ... Ribbentrop, at last shorn of his arrogance and pompousness, looking pale, bent and beaten ... Julius Streicher, the Jew-baiter of Nuremberg was there. This sadist and pornographer, whom I had once seen striding through the streets of the old town brandishing a whip, seemed to have wilted. A bald, decrepit-looking old man, he sat perspiring profusely glaring at the judges and convincing himself – so a guard told me later – that they were all Jews.'

Seven of the Nuremberg defendants – Hess, Raeder, Funk, Speer, Schirach, Neurath and Doenitz – received varying prison sentences. Eleven were sentenced to death, but only ten of them went to the

Dame Laura Knight's overall impression of the Nuremberg defendants in the dock and, stretching beyond the courtroom, the ruins of Europe.

gallows on 16 October 1946. Goering cheated the hangman by swallowing a vial of poison which he had concealed in his cell. Three of the defendants – the foxy diplomat von Papen, the economist Schacht and Goebbels' pathetic subordinate Fritzsche – were acquitted at Nuremberg and then handed over to denazification courts for trial and sentence. Nuremberg was the centrepiece of Allied attempts to fix the guilt for the horrors and suffering of the Second World War. Its jurisprudential basis remains open to doubt, and A.J.P. Taylor voiced an uncomfortable view when he wrote, 'a few German leaders were hanged after a sort of trial – mainly for the crime of having lost.' He continued, 'Apart from this, it was soon assumed that, while the atrocious crimes were being committed, all the Germans, except Hitler, were somewhere else.'

In the British and American zones the authorities went through the motions. The Americans issued twelve million forms containing 131 questions about the subject's past life and associations. In the western zones, just under 170,000 individuals were put on trial for their wartime activities. Nevertheless, the awkward fact remained that if the zones were to be restored to a semblance of economic order, reliance would have to be placed on former members of the Nazi Party or Nazi sympathizers. In October 1946 the Saturday Evening Post published an article about the steel trust in the American zone: 'To be precise, of the 361 top executives who were members of the Nazi Party, only 33 have been arrested.' Alfred Krupp, the industrialist who had headed the largest Nazi arms organization, was originally sentenced by a US court to 12 years imprisonment. Within three years he was back at the head of his trust.

With the right connections, a former Nazi who wished to flee abroad could obtain a false International Red Cross passport, an entry visa to a foreign country and, ultimately, a job in an emigré German community. This escape route was used by Franz Stangl, the former

Defendants at Nuremberg, 22 November 1945. Front row from left, Goering, Ribbentrop, Keitel, Rosenberg. Back row, Doenitz, Raeder, von Schirach, Sauckel, Jodl. Hess is missing from his usual seat beside Goering.

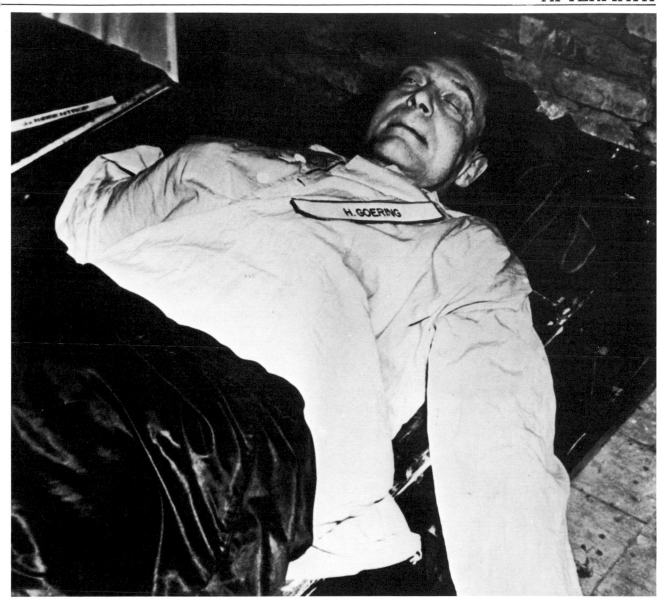

below left and above
Nuremberg provided
Goering, slimmed down and
weaned off morphine, with
the platform for a final
bravura display. On 16
October in his cell he
swallowed a poison capsule
which turned his corpse pale
green. Along with the others
who were executed after the
trial his body was
incinerated in the freshly lit
ovens of Dachau. The ashes
were scattered in the Isar
river.

commandant of Treblinka, who escaped from an Austrian open prison
in 1948 and made his way via Syria to Brazil. He was finally extradited
from Sao Paolo in 1967. Adolf Eichmann, the man who as head of the
Gestapo's Section IV BG had been responsible for the implementation
of the 'Final Solution to the Jewish Problem', had been imprisoned
after the war but not identified. He escaped in 1946, lived for four years
near Hamburg, working as a lumberjack, and then found his way to
Rome where a sympathetic priest gave him a refugee passport in the
name of Riccardo Clement. In 1960 he was discovered by Israeli
agents in Buenos Aires and kidnapped. He was put on trial in Israel,
found guilty and hanged.

The ultimate failure of denazification is to be found in the case of
Klaus Barbie, the 'Butcher of Lyons', who had been responsible for the
torture and death of many members of the French Resistance,
including one of its leading figures, Jean Moulin. After the war he fell
into American hands, and in the Cold War climate of 1947
counter-intelligence agents found a use for him, supplying them with
information about French Communists who had fought with the
Resistance. The United States resisted all efforts to extradite Barbie to
France to stand trial, and in 1950 assisted his flight to Bolivia.

AFTERMATH
FRATERNIZATION

When the first American troops crossed the Rhine, they carried with them pamphlets which strictly forbade contact with any Germans outside the requirements of duty. The punishment for fraternization with the enemy was a $65 fine – a month's pay for a GI. The forces' magazine Stars and Stripes exhorted the troops, 'Don't Get Chummy With Gerry ... In Heart, Body and Spirit Every German is Hitler'.

After the German capitulation the non-fraternization order quickly broke down. Human nature proved too strong. In the town of Hamelin one of the members of the British military government team quickly realized, 'The only thing missing ... a very big one, is human company other than our own ... No one amongst us is likely to forget the Germans' guilt but there will come a time when the stony stare must give place to a reasonably human glance and the hand to be shaken in politeness if not in friendship. Most of us are looking forward to that day if only to be able to tell the Germans what we have been thinking of them all this time.'

In Austria, which had been left relatively untouched by war, it was difficult to remain aloof from the local population. A British corporal recalled, 'Of course we fratted. We chatted up the girls in our billets but if we invited them to come for a walk, we'd tell them to follow a hundred yards behind until we were out of sight of the village.' An American soldier felt the same way, 'No one could help it. The girls were pretty and they didn't wear much, and we'd been through hell, living hard, in the open.' A British soldier in Berlin was equally frank with Colonel Byford-Jones: '...of course quite a lot of us go to bed with the Fräuleins. They are nice and they are so well developed physically by sport... These girls will take any treatment and they treat you like a king – don't matter if you keep them waiting for half an hour – and they are thankful for little things, a bar of chocolate or a few fags! It's like giving these girls the moon, and they won't eat the chocolate until you stand over them!'

Clearing rubble in Essen.

The striking image of grain growing from an upturned German helmet belies the enormous problems facing the occupying forces in the immediate aftermath of the war.

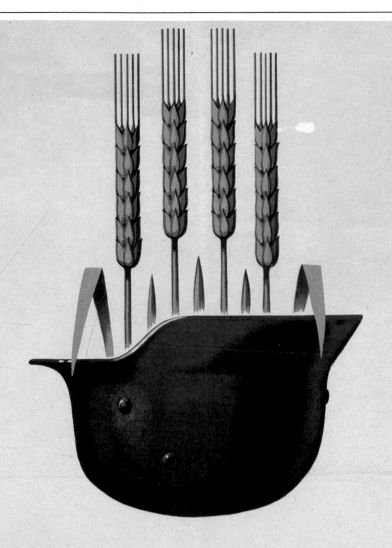

LESLIE
REECE

GERMANY
under control
EXHIBITION

OXFORD STREET **JUNE 7 – JULY 21**
(Tottenham Court Road end)

10 A.M. – **9** P.M. WEEKDAYS **1** P.M. – **9** P.M. SUNDAYS

Men look on while women work on cleaning up the Reichstag, its walls covered with graffiti left by Russian soldiers.

In July 1945 it became permissible to talk to German adults, but it was still forbidden to sit with them on park benches, to hold their hands or to enter their homes. In September troops in the American and British sectors were permitted 'normal human contacts', although marriage to Germans still remained forbidden, and it would be more than a year before Americans were allowed into German cinemas or Germans into American snack bars.

FUGITIVES AND DISPLACED PERSONS

The problems of fraternization paled into insignificance in comparison with those presented by 'displaced persons', known to everyone as DPs. In the British zone alone, in the summer of 1945 there were at least one million displaced persons – among them former slave labourers, released prisoners of war, and Germans ejected from the east.

For two weeks in May a hated figure slipped unrecognized into this human tide. On 5 May, at Flensburg, Heinrich Himmler held his last staff conference. Although Hitler's political testament had stripped

Heinrich Himmler lies dead on the floor of the British checkpoint at Bremervörde on 23 May after taking poison when stopped and recognized.

him of all his offices, and at Flensburg he had been openly snubbed by Doenitz, Himmler still nursed fantasies of establishing a 'reformed' Nazi administration in Schleswig Holstein which would then negotiate with the Allies as a sovereign government. Hugh Trevor Roper has painted a sardonic picture of the twilight of Himmler's dwindling empire as, still surrounded by an immense retinue, the former Reichsfuehrer lingered on the outskirts of Flensburg: 'Like obsolete dinosaurs, moving inappropriately in the wrong geological age, they gathered at his headquarters – high SS and police leaders, Obergruppenfuehrer and Gruppenfuehrer, heads now of defunct organizations, sustained only by portentous titles, the memory of vanished authority and absurd illusions.'

The illusions were swiftly shattered. After the German capitulation Himmler's jellied powers of decision deserted him completely. He dithered, vacillated, drove aimlessly around the surrounding countryside, sometimes sleeping in station waiting rooms. Finally he set off on foot with his secretary and adjutant. To disguise himself he had shaved off his moustache and donned an eye patch. In his pocket he carried the papers of a man long since executed by the Nazis. He had no idea of where he was going, and at 2pm on 23 May he blundered into a British checkpoint at Bremervörde. Six hours later he was identified. He was stripped and searched and, as the Army doctor's fingers groped in his mouth, Himmler bit on the poison capsule concealed there. Fifteen minutes later he was dead. A blanket was thrown over his corpse and two days later he was buried in an unmarked grave.

Perhaps the final irony is that Himmler – the ultimate political blank – failed so dismally to melt into the anonymity of the columns of refugees and prisoners of war trudging through Germany. At the end of the war the film star David Niven was in Germany, serving as a colonel in the British Army. One morning he came across a 'hastily erected prisoner-of-war cage in the open country between Hanover and Osnabruck ... There must have been a hundred thousand men already inside. The first warming rays of the sun were just touching the prisoners. It had rained heavily during the night and now a cloud of steam was rising from this dejected field-grey mass of humanity.'

When they were released, many former prisoners of war put their military training to use, forming bands which roamed the countryside

On 28 May William Joyce – Lord Haw Haw – was captured when quite unnecessarily he engaged two British officers in conversation while out for a walk near his hiding place. One of the officers, suspecting that Joyce was reaching for a gun as he groped for his identity papers, shot him in the thigh. He stood trial for treason in London and was hanged on 3 January 1946.

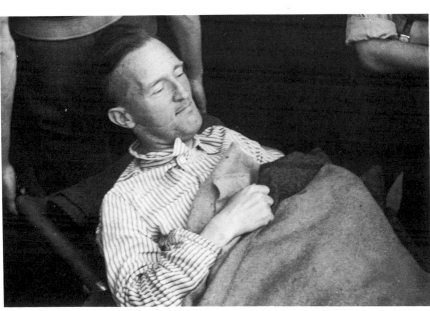

A painting by Anthony Gross of German refugees waiting to cross the bridge between Lauenburg and Bolzenburg in April 1945.

and, in some cases, linked up with other groups of displaced persons. Even the camps for the DPs run by UNRRA (the United Nations Relief and Rehabilitation Administration) could be dangerous places. This is a typical report from the British zone: 'It is unsafe to work in the fields within eight miles of Adelheide DP camp owing to sniping in this area. A total of 1,300 cattle have been slaughtered and looted by DPs and POWs, quite apart from atrocious crimes against the inhabitants.' Another officer in the military government wrote, 'I, on my frequent and long trips about our zone, always have a loaded pistol at hand, and my driver with a loaded rifle. Russians and Poles: Poles and Russians; and both worse than any kind of wild beast.'

The number of displaced persons in Germany had been swollen by the forced emigration of the German populations of eastern Europe. These people fell into three categories: *Lebensraum* Germans sent by Hitler to colonize the conquered territories in the east; the Reichsdeutsche, from the portions of Germany proper now occupied by the Red Army; and Volkdeutsche, ethnic Germans from Poland, Hungary and Czechoslovakia. This enormous migration had been under way since the autumn of 1944. Millions of people were involved – at the beginning of 1945 there were at least five million Germans in the Oder-Neisse region of Poland.

Article XII of the Potsdam Protocol gave a belated diplomatic gloss to this traumatic upheaval, recognizing that 'the transfer to Germany of German populations, and elements thereof, remaining in Poland, Czechoslovakia and Hungary will have to be undertaken'. In this 'undertaking' over two million people died, many of them beside the roads on to which they had been turned with little more than the clothes they stood up in.

This westward migration was balanced by a corresponding forced migration to the east of the 5.5 million Russians who had become prisoners of war and slave labourers, or who had deserted to the

opposite Edward Bawden's impression of a DP camp.

German refugees fleeing from the East find temporary shelter in Berlin.

enemy. Some two million remained in the zones controlled by the British and the Americans. Stalin wanted them back, and following Churchill and Eden's visit to Moscow in October 1944, the process began. About 10,000 Russians who had fallen into British hands in Normandy were shipped back to Murmansk from British ports. Most of them were marched straight off the ships and into penal battalions for the fighting in Poland and the assault on Berlin. The survivors returned to 25 years forced labour.

In Stalin's eyes there was little distinction to be made between those Russians who had fought for the Germans and those who had suffered terribly at their hands as prisoners of war. He allowed his own son Yakov to die as a German prisoner rather than exchange him for Hitler's nephew.

At Potsdam the British and Americans agreed to the forced repatriation of all Soviet citizens who were living within its borders in 1939. Most of these people knew the fate which awaited them. Others were blithely unaware of the plans the British and Americans were preparing. At the end of the war there were in the pleasant Drau valley, in Austria, over 50,000 Cossacks who had fought for Hitler, men of the Cossack Cavalry Corps, officered by White Russians, and the Cossack Division, under the command of the Russian-speaking Balt General von Pannwitz. They had flooded over the Austrian-

Members of the British military distributing food to displaced persons.

A German soldier wounded and captured at Stalingrad returns home to the West in 1947 after being released by the Russians as a disabled man. He is crossing the Anglo-Russian Demarkation Line near Lübeck.

Italian border from the Alpine region around Tolmezzo which, in happier days, Alfred Rosenberg had designated a Cossack 'homeland'. With their covered wagons, camels and thousands of camp followers – wives, children and priests – they seemed like a vision from the Thirty Years War.

The Cossack Division had served as lines of communications troops, but had seen no combat. The Cavalry Corps had been unleashed by their German masters in a bloody campaign against Tito's partisans. They were disarmed by the British, with whom they remained on friendly terms – their officers even competed against their British counterparts in a series of gymkhanas.

At the same time they seemed the least of the British worries. Hovering on the Austrian-Yugoslav border was an army of 200,000 Croatians. Lying in wait for the Croatians were Tito's partisans. They had scores to settle, as throughout the war Croatia had been governed as an independent fascist state. The British commander on the spot, Brigadier Scott of the 38th (Irish) Brigade, gave the Croatians three simple options: they could fight it out with the Titoists; they could advance on the British lines where they would be met with a heavy aerial and artillery bombardment (this was a calculated bluff); or they could surrender to the Titoists. The Croatians chose the third option. They surrendered to the Yugoslav partisans with the guarantee that the civilians would be sent back to Croatia and the soldiers treated as POWs, with the exception of 'political criminals'. It was an agreement unlikely to be honoured. As Scott remarked, 'I've no idea whether they were all murdered. I wouldn't be surprised if they were.'

After the Croatians it was the turn of the Cossacks. Between 28 May

A portrait from the German propaganda magazine *Signal* of Cossacks on the eastern front in 1943.

and 13 June they were handed over to the Russians by troops of the British Army. On 27 May the 1,500 officers of the Cossack Division were lured into attending a non-existent conference about their future at Oberdrauberg. The next day they were bundled into trucks and, under armed escort, driven to Judenburg, where the Red Army was waiting for them. When a British officer asked a Soviet soldier what would happen to the Cossacks, he 'just made a face and drew his finger across his throat'. Many of these Cossack officers had left Russia after the Revolution and thus fell outside the 1939 citizenship conditions laid down in the Potsdam Protocol.

At Lienz several thousand Cossack women and children formed themselves into a solid square protected by their menfolk. The square had to be broken up by rifle butts before the Cossacks were driven into the waiting trucks. Those who escaped into the surrounding countryside were diligently hunted down.

Of the 5.5 million Soviet citizens who were eventually repatriated it is estimated that about 20 per cent were sentenced to death or 25 years hard labour; another 15 to 20 per cent were given shorter terms of hard labour; 10 per cent were exiled to Siberia; 15 per cent were detailed to rebuild the Soviet Union's war-torn cities, and 15 per cent were allowed to go home; the remainder escaped or died in transit.

NEW HOPE FOR EUROPE

A relentless catalogue of destruction, death and deprivation can all too easily obscure the fact that in Europe in the summer of 1945 there was an upsurge of idealism and optimism. The continent had been grievously mauled but people sensed that they were waking from a long nightmare. Fascism had been defeated, and with liberation from the oppressor came a liberation from the dead hand of traditional authorities and reactionary politicians. Frank Thompson, a British Army officer, sensed this mood when in 1944 he wrote home from the Middle East: 'There is a spirit abroad in Europe which is freer and braver than anything that tired continent has known for centuries, and which cannot be withstood. You can, if you like, think of it in terms of politics, but it is broader and more generous than any dogma. It is the confident will of whole peoples, who have known the utmost humiliation and suffering and have triumphed over it, to build their own lives once and for all.'

Montgomery acknowledges the cheers of the people of Copenhagen, liberated on 5 May 1945 by a token force of his 21st Army Group.

In a Europe where both the familiar political and physical landmarks had been badly knocked about many shared Arthur Calder-Marshall's view that 'we are like men exploring the earth after a cataclysm, but with the old maps'. In the occupied countries of Europe, the pre-war authority of landowners, industrialists, and in some cases the church, had been undermined by the compromises they had made with fascism.

The Resistance movement had preserved a belief in human dignity and in a large measure provided the platform for hopes of postwar reconstruction. In turn these hopes were bound up with the strong transnational move to the Left which ran through Europe in the immediate postwar years. The author and Resistance member Albert Camus wrote, 'During all the time when we were obstinately and silently serving our country, we never lost sight of an idea and a hope forever present in us – the idea and hope of Europe.'

In the final year of the war the symbolic strength of the Resistance was translated into concrete military terms. In Italy, for example, the partisans were able to liberate well over 100 towns without Allied support. By the end of 1944 a broad-based anti-fascist coalition had been formed in Italy with four Communists on its central committee.

Many idealistic young officers serving in Europe with the British Army were deeply impressed by the achievements of the Resistance, seeing them as part of a wider movement towards a socialist Europe. Among them was the young Major Denis Healey, who returned from Italy to address the Labour Party conference in December 1944. Picture Post devoted a whole spread to Healey, singling him out as a 'Representative of Labour's Young Men'. 'The struggle for socialism in Europe', Healey told the conference, 'has been hard, cruel bitter and bloody ... After paying this price, our comrades won't let go.' He went on to describe how the war had 'liberated the virtues of the common people' and sat down to a rapturous storm of applause after lambasting the corrupt and decrepit bourgeoisie of Europe. It was an impressive political debut and it caught the mood of the conference just as much as it caught the Labour Party establishment off their guard.

By the autumn of 1944 the young lions of the Labour Party were chafing at their leaders' comfortable accommodation with the coalition administration. The war cabinet had avoided divisions along party lines and as Richard Casey, an Australian diplomat who attended a number of cabinet meetings, wrote, 'practically all the Labour Ministers integrate loyally and helpfully with the Tories, particularly Bevin.'

At the Labour Party conference there was a demonstration of the rank and file's increasing dissatisfaction with the leadership's remoteness and overly cautious approach to the planning of postwar Britain. A parliamentary candidate, Ian Mikardo, moved a resolution calling on the national executive to include in any future electoral manifesto 'the transfer to public ownership of the land, large-scale building, heavy industry and all forms of banking, transport, fuel and power'. The motion was passed on a clear show of hands.

Within three months the wartime political truce observed by the three main parties was beginning to break down. In March, at the Conservative party conference, Churchill attacked the Labour Party's proposals, claiming that they would destroy British society and impose a new system 'borrowed from foreign lands and alien minds.' It was Churchill's intention to detach the Labour leaders, particularly the Minister of Labour Ernest Bevin, from the clutches of their more

Prince Olaf returns to Norway after wartime service in the British forces.

militant supporters and entice them into a postwar coalition government. Bevin squashed the subsequent rumour and speculation in the press when, on 7 April, he addressed a Labour Party meeting in Yorkshire. He mounted a bitter attack on the pre-war record of the Conservative Party and angrily denied that he was about to step into the shoes of Ramsay MacDonald, the ghost at every Labour Party feast. He went on to list coal, fuel, power, steel and transport as industries fit for nationalization after the war. The gloves were now off and, to the dismay of many of the electorate, old-fashioned party welfare had emerged from its burrow after six years of hibernation.

POSTWAR BRITAIN

A month later Germany capitulated and the British found themselves confronting the brave new world hoped and planned for during the years of war. The bonfires which blazed on VE night heralded the end of many irksome restrictions. At the beginning of June the petrol ration for 'inessential' motoring was restored – four gallons a month for cars up to 8hp and five for those of 10-13hp. On 10 May the blackout regulations in the coastal regions were lifted. On the same day in the House of Commons Herbert Morrison announced the end of a long list of Defence Regulations, including the one which made it an offence to spread alarm and despondency. It was easier to abolish alarm than to dispel despondency. Many would have agreed with the young civil

opposite Men of 8th Army relax in Venice in the summer of 1945.

right Members of the services see some of the latest fashions at a London store in March 1945...

...but the reality of postwar Britain was to be found in endless queues and shortages. On a freezing January day in Fulham, west London, a long line forms for the distribution of children's woollen clothes from Australia.

servant at the Ministry of Supply who told Mass-Observation: 'Personally, although I was glad it was over, I was not particularly excited. For us, the dangerous-to-life part of the war ended just before Easter, when the rockets stopped. I was very relieved then. The Japanese have still to be finished off and materials for civil use are in such short supply, out of which we have to do our share in helping the countries of Europe, that I think we shall have very little change for some time.'

Victory had arrived, but the cupboard was almost bare. There was less meat in the shops than there had been a year before. In May the bacon ration was reduced from four ounces to three and the lard ration from two ounces to one. On 14 May the floodlighting of public buildings came to an end and, owing to the fuel shortage, all outdoor decoration and display lighting was discontinued. In September the clothing ration was cut to only 36 coupons a year.

On 21 May the British set out for the seaside to enjoy their first peactime Bank Holiday. Inevitably, it rained. The wind whistled through the promenade shelters, shabby from lack of paint and long since deprived of their glass windows. Buckets and spades had to be hired as none had been made during the war. The Daily Mail commented, 'Brighton tried to be its gay old self, but with most of the shops, cafés, amusements, public houses and hotels closed, it was impossible.' Even the beach was rationed, as most of it remained closed because of the danger from mines. It was to be another two months before Brighton's beaches were once again safe for bathers, and nearly a year before its two piers – both of which had been badly damaged – were open to the public.

Britain's long-term economic problems could not be moved as easily as the mines which cluttered the Brighton shingle. In a Treasury minute of 14 August – the day the Japanese surrendered – J.M. Keynes warned that Britain was facing 'a financial Dunkirk'. The war had exhausted her financial resources as early as 1941, but this had been largely disguised by the flow of goods and raw materials from the United States under the terms of the Lend-Lease agreement. When Lend-Lease came to an end in 1945, Britain found herself in a grave financial crisis. Her external debts had risen from the 1939 level of £496 million to £3,500 million. Her pre-war gold and dollar reserves had been dissipated, along with £1,118 million of overseas investments. Bankruptcy was avoided by a $4,000 million loan from the United States granted on tough terms which included the abandonment of the system of imperial preferences and an

The transport strike in the winter of 1946-7 forced Londoners to eke out their meat ration with horseflesh.

Cigarettes were in permanently short supply, although favoured customers could take advantage of the 'under-the-counter' stock.

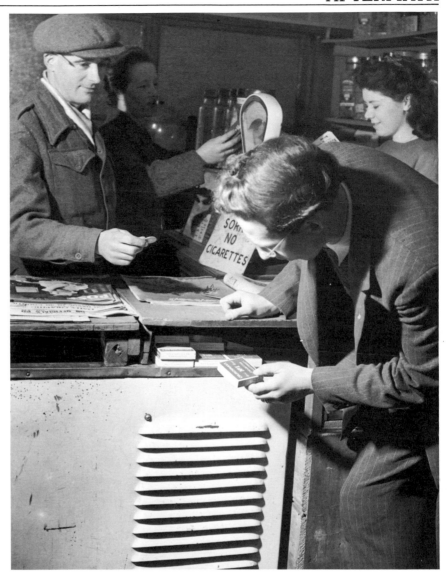

undertaking to restore the convertibility of sterling. (When this undertaking was fulfilled in 1947, it preciptated another financial crisis.)

Shipping losses had amounted to 18 million tons, of which only two thirds had been replaced. As many as four million houses, almost a third of the total stock, had been damaged by enemy action, including half a million totally destroyed. The housing shortage was one of the major preoccupations of the immediate postwar period. There were many complaints about the slow pace of repairs to damaged buildings. An outraged letter in the Westminster and Pimlico News pointed out that in May 1945 workmen were still repairing the bomb-damaged homes they had taken over after the Blitz: 'The workmen's Sunday pay is 4/5d an hour and all we see the men do is dawdle and drink cups of tea.'

The effects of Britain's wartime exertions were still being felt at the end of the decade and were reflected in the massive 1949 devaluation of sterling from $4.03 to $2.80. As Correlli Barnett has observed, the wartime operation of Lend-Lease transformed Britain into an American satellite warrior-state dependent for her existence on a supply chain which stretched across the Atlantic. The sheer brute strength of the American economy – whose GNP shot up by 60 per cent during the war – simply gobbled up its allies' requirements. In the course of the hostilities the United States provided civil and military aid to her allies on a scale that would have been sufficient for her to raise 2,000 infantry divisions. After the victory had been won Britain could not escape from her economic dependence on the United States.

On the credit side of the balance sheet was the modernization and reinvigoration of Britain's farming industry, a development foreshadowed in the late 1930s and accelerated by wartime planning and controls. Between 1938 and 1944 the total area of tilled land increased by five million acres and the total net output of calories was doubled. Yields were boosted by the increased use of fertilizers, the quadrupling of the number of tractors employed on farms, and a

opposite Wartime slogans were put to good use. The harvest of 1945 was disastrous throughout Europe.

Relics of wartime and postwar austerity.

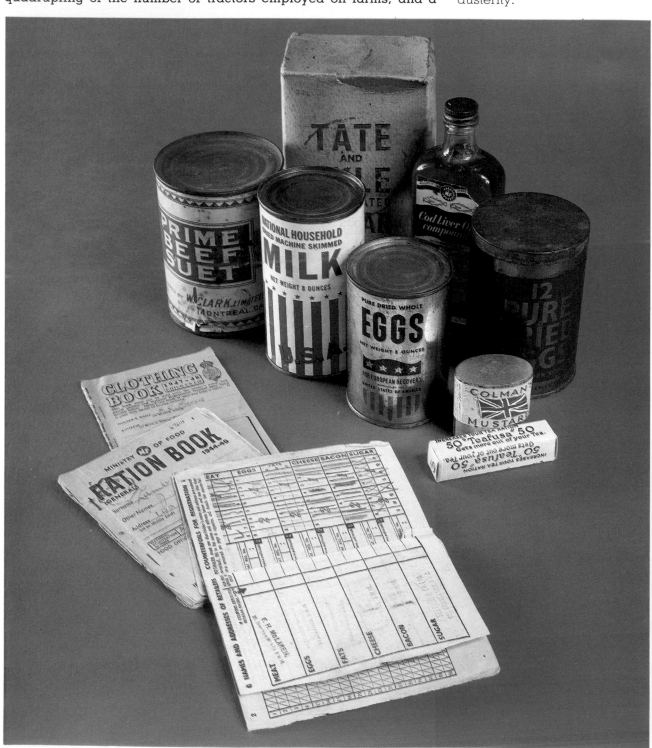

The need is 'GROWING'..

DIG FOR VICTORY STILL

far-reaching system of loans and subsidies. The war also acted as a powerful stimulus to industries which were to be vital to Britain's economic survival in the postwar years – motor vehicles, electronics, aircraft and chemicals. High-technology developments in radar, nuclear power, jet propulsion and antibiotics carved out an important role for science in British industry. However, the war, with its specialized and economically haphazard demands, had ensured that declining pre-war industries like shipbuilding, iron and steel were transformed into vital sectors of the war effort. In the years after 1945 this concentration of resources in industries which might otherwise have been obliged to decline resulted in a crucial distortion of the economy.

Despite the severities and sacrifices on the home front, the war brought many gains for working-class people and their families. There was full employment, wages kept well ahead of prices, and rationing, with its guarantee that essential fuels and goods reached everyone, ensured that for millions of people life was better throughout the war than it had been in the 1930s.

It was the impact of wartime planning on ordinary people's lives, and the practical benefits which flowed from it, that did most to change the political climate in Britain between 1940 and 1945. The measures taken to fight a 'total war' themselves transformed the

One of the many GI brides who chose to try their luck across the Atlantic. Showgirl Irene Taylor at her marriage on 19 May to Captain Oscar O'Neill of the USAAF, recently returned from Stalag Luft 3 in Germany.

'Demob is the only subject of any conversation. The first thing you ask any newcomer is his demob number.' Details of demobilization were released by the government in September 1944. The scheme created two classes for demobilization: Class B covered builders and others urgently required for postwar reconstruction – they would have priority of release, but would be recalled if they left the work to which they had been directed. The remainder – Class A – were to be demobilized according to a plan which took into account both age and length of service. Two month's service were counted as the equivalent of a year in age, so that a man of 22 with four year's service had the same release date priority as a man of 40 with one year's service.

context of the debate about the social policy to be pursued in peacetime. The adoption of J.M. Keynes' policies in the War Budget of 1941 ensured that the problem of war finance was seen not merely in budgetary terms but as a question of the deployment of the total economic resources of the nation. As a result state control was extended to embrace almost every aspect of Britain's economic and social life.

The process had already begun in 1939 with the establishment of the Emergency Hospital System, when the 1930s patchwork of private and health insurance schemes was found to be wholly inadequate to meet the demands of wartime. The hated 'means test', applied as a check on the household income of those in need, was abolished in 1941. The Assistance Board brought a degree of humanity to the provision of help for the victims of bomb damage and service families claiming allowances. No longer were they treated as troublesome supplicants to whom charity was grudgingly administered. Help was now provided solely on the basis of human need. In July 1940 a programme of free school milk was set up to protect children against the ill-effects of rationing and this was followed by the provision of orange juice, cod liver oil and vitamin tablets. Working women were assisted by the introduction of free school meals and nurseries. By the autumn of 1943 some 2,000 British Restaurants were serving over 600,000 hot meals a day, providing good food at a shilling a head.

As early as July 1942 the Political and Economic Planning Group had published a broadsheet – *Planning for Social Security* – calling for a national minimum income, universal family allowances, a National Health Service and a Ministry of Social Security. This

---

DAILY EXPRESS

No. 14,020   Lighting-up time: 10.40 pm to 5.12 am   SATURDAY MAY 12 1945   Moon rises 6.56 am sets 10.36 pm   One Penny

RELEASING THE TROOPS IS EXPECTED TO BEGIN FIVE WEEKS FROM MONDAY
Firms to submit names of key men they need urgently on the job

FIRST DEMOB. DAY—JUNE 18

200,000 in Forces likely to be freed

FAR EAST EXEMPTIONS

Express Industrial Reporter

PROVISIONAL date for the start of demobilisation has been fixed. It is Monday, June 18. No final decision has yet been taken, but it is hoped that the first 11 groups of men in Class A—about 200,000 men—will be released on that day.

At one time it was hoped that Groups 1—25 inclusive would be released together, but it now seems unlikely that first demobilisation will get beyond Group 11.

Groups 1—11 include men over 50 who have first priority of release whatever date they were called up, and everyone over 41 who was called up before September 1941.

The rate at which demobilisation will go on after June 18 will depend mainly on the military situation in the Far East, on decisions about the policing and occupation of Germany, and on the numbers becoming available in the new conscription groups.

In accordance with the policy of fairness to older men with long service, those in Groups 1—27 (that is, men over 25 called up in the earlier stages of the war) will not be sent to the Far East.

A full and official statement is expected on Wednesday, when the whole question of demobilisation and resettlement is to be debated in the House of Commons.

GETTING LISTS

AMERICA HONOURS THE DAILY EXPRESS

Express Staff Reporter

COLUMBIA (Missouri), Friday.—The Daily Express was today accorded a distinctive American honour. Every year the University of Missouri's School of Journalism, one of the finest in the world, asks a committee of America's most prominent newspapermen to report to them the outstanding foreign newspaper. This year they chose the Daily Express.

To the London Daily Express in recognition of its leadership throughout its history in the dynamic display of news; in admirable example in the field of architecture for newspaper plants; its supremacy in circulation ...

THIS IS HOW MOSCOW WELCOMED THE BRITISH ON VE DAY

LOOK at the faces here and see how Russia reacted to the Peace. Men, women boys, girls are wild with joy. Hundreds of thousands of them flocked into Moscow for the VE Day festival. They sang they danced. And any Allied Serviceman they met was given an ovation that left him staggered by his welcome. ...

COVENTRY WAS MY WORK

GOERING ADMITS IT

From WILLIAM TROUGHTON, Seventh U.S. Army, Friday

IT was Goering who ordered the bombing of Coventry. He admitted it today clearly and without equivocation to more than 40 war reporters.

He was asked : "Did you order the bombing of Coventry?"

He hesitated for a spat, seemed and then replied emphatically, "Jawohl" (Yes, of course).

He hesitated again, and then added : "I ordered the attack against Coventry because ...

THE MYSTERY OF 17 DAYS
WHERE

Churchill may hint at election date

By GUY EDEN

MR. CHURCHILL may give an indication of the date of the general election in his broadcast tomorrow night.

It may either be at the end of next month or early July, or ...

MEAT RATION WILL BE CUT
Method not yet decided

Express Food Reporter KENNETH PIPE

BRITAIN'S rations will have to be cut as a result of the world food shortage. That is now certain; but how and when the cut will be made is not decided.

Colonel Llewellin, Food Minister ...

Jap peace feelers

'Keep out of our homeland'

WASHINGTON, Friday.—Rumours of Japanese peace offers circulated in Washington today.

The Japs, however, have made nothing like an offer ...

4 a.m. LATEST
JAP ENVOY CAPTURED

SEVENTH ARMY Saturday.—Jap Ambassador to Germany General Hiroshi Oshima, 129 officials and 170 Embassy staff have been captured. They include Nazi Envoy Minister Dr Walter von Etzdorf.

GERMAN SECRET MISSION ARRIVES

German naval officers sent to Scotland and 170 are taken warships in the Firth to disinfected secrets.

unconditional surrender—to the Allies.

anticipated by five months the publication of the Beveridge Report, whose recommendations crystallized the movement towards social reform. The autumn of 1942 proved to be a watershed in the development of public opinion. As Howard Spring wrote in the September 1942 edition of St Martin's Review, 'I think there was a breach, for some time before the war, between what the people wanted and what the politicians were doing. It was the sense of the widening of the breach that produced the dreadful feeling of frustration in so many minds. If ever again comes the chance of thinking about these things, we shall have to ask ourselves how may this be avoided. Throughout the war – like the seed growing secretly – the thinking had been done and the private questions asked.'

The government, prompted by the Ministry of Information, recognized this fact, and the heightening of postwar expectations was itself incorporated into the war-winning strategy. The Beveridge Report was by no means a revolutionary document. Its aim was to

opposite Guests at Butlin's Holiday Camp at Filey, Yorkshire, aboard a Bren gun carrier.

Holidaymakers return to the beach at Hastings in August. Clearing Britain's coasts of mines and obstacles was a major headache that summer.

unify and extend the *existing* measures for social security, the product not of a socialist but, as Aneurin Bevan pointed out, that of an 'honest Liberal' (Beveridge was a pillar of the Liberal Party). Nevertheless, the Report was received with overwhelming interest and enthusiasm. Eventually over 600,000 copies were sold, including a big printing for the United States. Most significantly, an opinion poll revealed that although only about half the professional and white collar classes thought that they would benefit from the Report, nine out of ten of them supported its immediate implementation. In the same poll only three out of ten in the highest income bracket thought that they would benefit from Beveridge, but three quarters of them felt that it should be adopted.

The pure essence of Beveridgeism was found in the Common Wealth party. Founded in 1942 by a merger of J.B. Priestley's 1941 Committee and the Forward March Movement, it provided a focus for the middle-class idealism of the period, sardonically characterized by Paul Addison as 'Colonel Blimp being pursued through a land of Penguin Specials by an abrasive meritocrat, a progressive churchman and J.B. Priestley'. Combining a rather windy and generalized radicalism with such notions as 'common ownership', 'vital democracy' and 'morality in politics', Common Wealth never possessed more than 15 thousand members. Nevertheless it won two

By the end of 1945 about 30,000 demobbed men a week were turning to the Resettlement Advice Service for help in their return to civilian life. Meanwhile demobilization ground on into 1946, prompting a shortlived 'demob strike' by RAF personnel in the Far East.

remarkable wartime by-election victories, the first of which, in April 1943 in the rural constituency of Eddisbury, Cheshire, was won on a platform of 'Beveridge In Full Now', the nationalization of agriculture and the opening of a second front.

The Beveridge Report was just one, albeit the most important, of the proliferation of reports and White Papers which anticipated the end of the war and mapped out the courses of action for postwar planning. The Scott Report (1942) dealt with the control of rural development. The Uthwatt Report (1942) proposed the nationalization of land values and control on the siting of new factories. A White Paper on Employment, published in 1944, pledged the government to a policy of ensuring full employment. The Palache Report (1944) considered the future role of the film industry, which had undergone a dramatic revival during the war. Even the Jockey Club got in on the act, appointing a committee – including three peers and a knight – to look into horse racing. Its recommendations included cheaper and better accommodation for the race-going public.

In all this the British people were not simply the grateful recipients of bureaucratic largesse, led by their noses through a steady drizzle of White Papers drafted by high-minded civil servants. At the beginning of the conflict Mass-Observation had reported that the prevailing mood was one of 'This is not our war – this is a war of the high-ups who use long words and have different feelings'. Total war – with its shared hardships and sacrifices – brought with it a remarkable degree of collective solidarity. It also opened many people's eyes to

This extract from a serviceman's diary covers some of the events of the day of his demobilization in March 1946. After an exasperating six-hour wait at the Civilian Clothing Depot he finally got the chance to choose his 'demob' suit: 'Here it is – this is the last stop – now I'm not going to be hurried. Take your time, pick something good – see if it creases. H'm not bad, but what, only these? Try the next size; ah, these are better ... If only Phyllis were here ... Everyone else looks just as worried. Oh damn, I don't know – where was that first one? This? Ah, a trenchcoat – fine. What cheap shirts and what lousy ties! ... The suit looks good and the shoes are rather utility.' Later our diarist expressed some remorse at choosing a brown suit after all those years in khaki.

Homecoming. Private Bill
Martin returns home to Kilburn,
north-west London, in
December, after serving with
the Royal Army Medical Corps
in Burma.

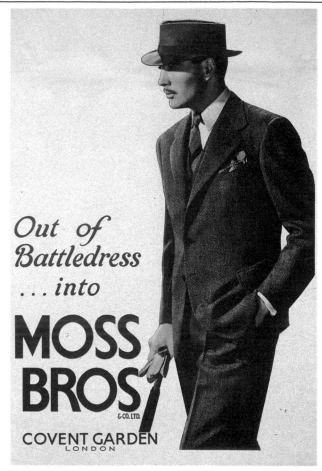

above For returning officers, Moss Bros had the solution.

above left and opposite Returned POWs were bombarded with advice on how to start afresh in Civvy Street.

left British POWs get a meal in a hangar at Brussels airport while waiting to be flown home. The painting is by Anne Katrina Zinkeisen.

the real state of the nation. Evacuation, the single most significant social upheaval of the war, brought home to prosperous professionals the extent of poverty in Britain. Even the 'high-ups' were not immune. Neville Chamberlain wrote in a private letter of September 1939, 'I never knew such conditions existed, and I feel ashamed of having been so ignorant of my neighbours.'

Public opinion frequently ran ahead of the government. Food rationing was not introduced until January 1940, although opinion

polls had shown a big majority in favour of its introduction from the outbreak of the war. On the one hand the British submitted to a mobilization of manpower that, with the possible exception of the Soviet Union, was the most comprehensive of all the combatant nations. On the other, the *voluntary* element in the war effort was reflected in the 1.5 million who enrolled in the Home Guard in the summer of 1940 and the thousands who served in the Air Raid Precaution (ARP). During the Blitz the big East End shelters – some of which housed up to 10,000 people – became 'little republics', electing their own delegates and shelter marshals and organizing their own canteens and clinics. As Ritchie Calder observed, the pressures of

American troops set sail for the United States aboard the Queen Mary. The use of one of Britain's biggest passenger ships for the transport of US personnel caused a great deal of resentment among British troops waiting to be shipped home from overseas.

collective effort were releasing creativity and resources which had been wasted or ignored in the 1930s. The inarticulate were becoming increasingly articulate.

In turn this generated an almost voracious interest in current affairs and public debate. Up and down the country the deliberations of the BBC's Brains Trust were imitated in the National Fire Service discussion schemes and the Industrial Discussion Clubs. For perhaps the first and only time this century left-wing and radical publications found a huge popular market. Harold Laski's *Where Do We Go From Here?*, a Penguin Special of 1940, sold 80,000 copies. After the entry into the war of the Soviet Union, Beatrice Webb's *Soviet Communism –*

A New Civilisation became one of a number of unlikely best-sellers.

An even wider audience was reached by the Daily Mirror newspaper, which championed the cause of the ordinary soldier, particularly in the agony column 'Question Time in the Mess', edited by a young journalist called Barbara Betts, who as Barbara Castle was later to become a Labour cabinet minister. The Mirror, with a

British ex-POWs captured at Arnhem catch their first glimpse of England from a transport flying them home.

PICTURE POST

THE FIRST SIGHT OF ENGLAND
Prisoners Taken at Arnhem Fly Home
(See inside)

HULTON'S NATIONAL WEEKLY

In this issue:

HOMECOMING

4D

MAY 12, 1945

Vol. 27. No. 6

circulation of 2.5 million, was popular journalism at its best – zesty, iconoclastic and taking its readership extremely seriously. Philip Zec's brilliant cartoons in The Mirror showed ordinary soldiers, merchant seamen and working people as resolute, heroic figures, more human versions of the jut-jawed Stakhanovites of Soviet social realism. The communicators' changing presentation of working people was also evident in Ealing films like *The Foreman Went to France* (1942), in which the hero of the title was a mature, cool-headed figure constantly at odds with the smug incompetence of those in authority. The gormless working-class stereotype personified by George Formby was increasingly out of step with the times, and although Formby's films remained popular through the mid-war years, his screen career came to an abrupt end shortly after the war with *George in Civvy Street* (1947).

Political debate among the troops was channelled through the Army Bureau of Current Affairs (ABCA), founded in August 1941 by the new Adjutant-General Sir Ronald Adam. Adam believed that, in a modern democracy, it was the soldier's right and duty to 'reason why'. Some of ABCA's improving flavour can be gauged from the experience of a young officer in France shortly after D-Day. Ducking into a barn to take cover from a German mortar bombardment, he found a corporal and twelve men earnestly discussing 'What Shall We Do With the Germans After the War'.

The War office kept a close eye on the radical tone of ABCA's lectures and discussions. In January 1943 the ABCA summary of the Beveridge Report was withdrawn without any explanation. In April 1944 the Cairo forces' 'parliament' was dissolved by the military authorities after it had passed a motion in favour of the nationalization of the banks. Blimpish senior officers may have seen this as tantamount to treason. What they could not see was that this was the spontaneous expression of a more general change taking place in the thinking of the troops abroad and civilians at home.

The Queen meets repatriated POWs at a garden party at Buckingham Palace in May 1945.

AFTERMATH

THE ELECTION

By the end of the war in Europe the political and social consciousness of the great majority of the British people was higher than at any time before or since. This mood provided the background to the election of July 1945. After discussions with Attlee, Churchill presented the coalition with two choices. Either it should continue until the end of the war in the Pacific – a prospect which still seemed about 18 months away; or it should be disbanded immediately and an election held in July. To complicate matters, Churchill also suggested that a referendum on the matter might be held. The Labour and Liberal leaderships – both of which had failed fully to discern the public mood – were extremely reluctant to agree to an immediate election, fearing a repeat of Lloyd George's 'Khaki Election', which would return Churchill as Prime Minister with a handsome majority. Attlee and Bevin urged the Labour Party National Executive Council (NEC) to accept Churchill's offer of a continued coalition, but they were voted down and the NEC's decision was endorsed in Blackpool by the Labour Party conference. Also rejected was the idea of a referendum, and Attlee's reply to Churchill contained the astringent observation that a referendum had 'only too often been the instrument of Nazidom and Fascism'. It was the opening shot in what was to become an increasingly bitter campaign.

Churchill tendered his resignation to the King on 23 May and a caretaker government, principally composed of Conservatives, stepped into the place of the coalition. Parliament was dissolved on 15 June. Meanwhile the election campaign got under way.

After the long political truce the nation gingerly flexed its political muscles. As the New Statesman commented: 'Six years of war have stiffened our political joints. Election tactics and procedure are a novelty to millions. Most citizens under 30 have never been called on to vote, and the older electors have only known nine years of Party government since 1916.'

There was some confusion in compiling the new register, which was compounded by wartime movements and evacuations and the creation of 25 new constituencies. Woodford was one of the new constituencies and its Conservative candidate, one Winston Churchill, found himself without a vote. He was not on the electoral roll for his home at Westerham, for Chequers or for Downing Street. Churchill had been out of the country in the summer of 1943 when the buff identity cards from which the register was compiled were exchanged for new ones. A new card had been issued for the Prime Minister, but the old one had not been handed in and thus he was disenfranchized.

There were nearly 1,700 candidates contesting 640 seats, including 306 Liberals, 23 Common Wealth candidates and 21 Communists. Attlee, with characteristic caution, reckoned that Labour's chances were 'no more than fair'. Hugh Dalton foresaw a Tory majority of 80, while Churchill's advisers predicted that he would be returned as Prime Minister with a majority of about 30. None of them set any store by the Gallup Poll in the News Chronicle, which had shown a Labour lead since 1943. Many party professionals believed that the election would provide little more than a relief from wartime austerity. The Liberal agent at Ilford, bemused by a huge crowd crammed into a hall to hear Sir Archibald Sinclair declare Sir William Beveridge 'a new prophet of Israel', was uncertain whether the audience was there 'out of a concern for politics or as a treat to go out to an evening meeting after all these years'.

Ernest Bevin bends ponderously to perform a time-honoured political ritual – the kissing of babies.

The experts had failed to read the signs, and none more so than the Conservatives. The Tory Party was in no shape to fight an election. Its constituency organization had been allowed to decay and Churchill's lack of interest in domestic issues had inhibited the development of a distinctively Tory approach to the issues raised by Beveridge. As a result the Tory and Labour programmes displayed a considerable overlap. Progressive Conservatives like Harold Macmillan and R.A. Butler, architect of the 1944 Education Act, realized that in order to survive as a political force their party had to take on board a commitment to a comprehensive housing programme, the introduction of a national health service and a national insurance scheme. But these were not policies with which the Party as a whole seemed comfortable. Churchill had clearly regarded Beveridge as a distraction from the prosecution of the war rather than a contribution towards it. Many of the electorate remained unconvinced that the Conservatives were willing to implement Beveridge other than in a watered-down form, a suspicion reinforced by the Tories' continued association in the public mind with appeasement and the mass unemployment of the 1930s. The point was driven home by books like Tom Wintringham's *Your MP*, which contained a damning list of pre-war statements made by the Conservative MPs on such topics as Hitler, Mussolini and the Means Test.

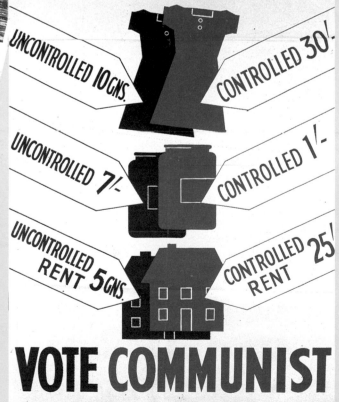

Posters for the 1945 election. Labour's, in the style of the Daily Mirror's Philip Zec, cleverly twists the Conservative slogan 'Let Him [Churchill] Finish The Job'. Neither of the Tory posters mentions the Conservative Party, relying instead on the appeal of the wartime coalition and the personal appeal of Winston Churchill. The Communist poster is rather more specific.

The Conservatives' principal asset was Churchill, but this proved a double-edged sword. As a contemporary commentator observed, 'Mr Churchill laid before the electors his manifold experience and asked for a renewal of their confidence, saying little or nothing of the Conservative Party.' The Tories' most familiar poster in the campaign did not even bear the name of their party but carried the legend, 'Vote National – Help Him finish the Job', under a pugnacious image of The Man With The Big Cigar. In the words of Angus Calder, 'Like naked heathens, they proclaimed the unique virtues of their tribal idol, a man whom most of them had spurned and ignored in the 1930s. The irony was not missed.'

In similar fashion the Tory manifesto was entitled *Mr Churchill's Declaration of Policy to the Electors* and contained a woolly restatement of his Four-Year Plan, the outlines of which he had broadcast as early as March 1943. Eschewing Churchill's presidential style, the Labour Party manifesto, *Let Us Face the Future*, did not mention Mr Attlee's name once. A crisply written document, leaning heavily on a sturdy managerialism which was more concerned with economic efficiency than with socialist dogma, it conveyed the impression that the Labour Party was more at home than the Tories in the new world of planning and government controls.

Churchill's dominating, theatrical style tended to overshadow his rather colourless team. Labour had the advantage of presenting a group of lively, well-contrasted figures well-known to the public through their service in the wartime coalition: the massive Bevin, jaunty Herbert Morrison, the voluble Hugh Dalton and the ascetic Stafford Cripps, high priest of austerity. In contrast with Churchill's grandiose national motorcades, there was something reassuring about Attlee's progress round the hustings in a modest family saloon driven by his wife. Attlee, brisk and modest to the point of monosyllables – the archetypal wartime committee man – seemed the embodiment of the self-effacing virtues of austerity Britain. The crowds came to cheer Churchill, but many of them went home intending to vote Labour.

At the end of the war Churchill had gloomily pondered with Lord Moran his imminent estrangement from the British people – 'I have nothing to tell them now.' As if to confirm that with the arrival of peace he had begun to lose his political bearings, Churchill opened the first party political broadcast of the campaign on 4 June with an astonishing blunder. He told his listeners, 'from the bottom of my heart ... no socialist system can be established without a political police.' If the Labour leaders tried to implement a fully socialist programme, 'They would have to fall back on some form of Gestapo, no doubt very humanely directed in the first instance.' Listening to the broadcast in the Carlton Club a young Tory candidate, Quintin Hogg, declared that the speech had cost the Conservatives at least a quarter of a million votes. Many diehard Tories were distressed by this manifest error of judgement. Writing to Harold Nicolson, Vita Sackville-West asked of Churchill, 'What has gone wrong with him?'

Of Churchill's 'Gestapo' broadcast Attlee mildly remarked, 'The voice we heard last night was that of Mr Churchill, but the mind was that of Lord Beaverbrook.' In fact Beaverbrook had little if any influence over Churchill's speeches, but his newspapers conveyed a different impression. On the morning of 5 June the Daily Express trumpeted, 'GESTAPO IN BRITAIN IF SOCIALISTS WIN – They would dictate what to say, and do, even where to queue.' Beaverbrook's newspapers continued in the same hysterical vein throughout the campaign. The Evening Standard printed a photograph of Labour's NEC – about as harmless-looking a bunch as one could imagine – with the accompanying caption, 'These People Want to be Dictators. Study Their Faces'.

A doomed attempt was made to brand the chairman of Labour's NEC, the garrulous Harold Laski, as a bloody revolutionary, and there was a hint of anti-semitism in references to his 'foreign–sounding' name. This only made Harold Macmillan's decision to dub Laski 'Gauleiter' even more foolish – a rare example of that master operator's faulty judgement.

At an election meeting at Stratford in East London, a Tory speaker, G.D. Roberts, told the audience, 'Are we going to have a Labour Party saying what we are going to do, directed by the hidden hand of Mr Laski?' After prolonged protests, he pressed on, singling out a particularly vociferous heckler. 'A man like you ... is not fit to have a vote. I have seen your kidney before. I expect you were shouting "Open a Second Front now" as though it were a tin of sardines and then went on strike.' The heckler then reminded G.D. Roberts that he had been bombed out in the Blitz like many another East Ender – 'some of the finest people in the world'. He added, 'The best thing you can do in fairness to your candidate is to sit down. I am not a Labour Party member or a Bolshie. I am just a common working man and I don't want to be insulted by you or by anyone else.'

The campaign ended on a sour note. Herbert Morrison, who had given up his safe East End seat to fight what was considered a marginal in Lewisham, revealed that in 1944 he had personally countermanded an order by Churchill that no warning should be given of the approach of individual V-1s. There had been a particularly horrible V-1 incident in Lewisham. Churchill came down to Lewisham on the eve of the poll and accused his former Home Secretary of running away from a Communist candidate. On the same night, in Tooting, someone had thrown a squib at Churchill which nearly exploded in his face.

THE RESULT

Polling day, 5 July, dawned warm and sunny. It was to be one of the hottest days of the month, and in Scotland the temperature crept up to 75°F. The national average poll was 70 per cent. Servicemen were allowed to claim a postal vote or to appoint a proxy. Because of the delay in gathering and counting their votes the announcement of the result was delayed until 26 July. Meanwhile Churchill and Attlee flew to the Potsdam conference where, at a military parade, Attlee was more warmly applauded by the troops than Churchill.

The press, Conservative Central Office and the Stock Exchange were still confident of a Tory victory, but on the night of 25 July, after flying back from Potsdam, Churchill had another premonition. He found it hard to sleep and 'just before dawn ... woke suddenly with a sharp stab of almost physical pain. A hitherto subconscious conviction that we were beaten broke forth and dominated my mind.'

At 9am on the following morning Churchill repaired to his old wartime map room where the election results were displayed on the walls. They made depressing reading. The first declaration had been at South Salford and, ominously, had been a Labour gain. Then the results came in a flood, and by 11am two cabinet ministers – Harold Macmillan and Brendan Bracken – had lost their seats. Soon afterwards Herbert Morrison was returned at Lewisham with a massive majority. Hard on the heels of Morrison's triumph came the

Attlee with his new government
in the garden of No 10.

A twist in political fortunes produces a reversal in style. An uncharacteristically ebullient Clement Attlee on hearing that Labour's lead is now unassailable; and a subdued Churchill leaving No 10 with his wife Clementine.

biggest shock of all: an eccentric independent, Mr Alexander Hancock, who had stood against Churchill at Woodford – where the Labour and Liberal Parties had decided not to oppose him – had polled 10,000 votes. As Churchill observed, 'By now it was clear that the socialists would have a majority. At luncheon my wife said to me, "It may well be a blessing in disguise". I replied, "At the moment it seems quite effectively disguised".'

At 7pm Churchill went to the King to tender his resignation. A little later Clement Attlee arrived, 'looking very surprised indeed' according to the King, to kiss the monarch's hand. By the end of the evening the scale of the Labour victory had become clear. When all the results were in, Labour had gained an overall majority of 146 with 393 seats, a net gain of 212 seats, many of which were sending a Labour MP to Parliament for the first time. The Tories and their allies had been reduced to 213 seats and the Liberals to 12. The Liberal leader, Sir Archibald Sinclair, had lost his seat, as had 29 members of the caretaker government, including 13 of cabinet rank. The Common Wealth Party had been all but wiped off the map. It lost its deposit in 16 of the seats it contested and its only success was at Chelmsford. A year later their man took the Labour whip.

The vagaries of the British electoral system had resulted in a Labour landslide, but the Tory vote held up quite well, polling 9,950,809 to the combined Labour/Liberal total of 14,232,292. After the war a myth grew up about the 'decisive' nature of the service vote, possibly prompted by General Slim's remark to Churchill that 90 per cent of the troops in Burma would vote Labour and the other ten would not vote at all. In fact, of the 2,895,000 with their names on the special services register, only 1,701,000 cast their votes. Crucial to Labour's success were the inroads it had made into the middle-class vote and a big increase in working-class support.

Churchill continued to maintain an outwardly philosophical attitude towards his defeat. When on the afternoon of the 26th Lord Moran spoke out against the 'ingratitude of the people', Churchill – sunk deep in gloom – roused himself to reply, 'Oh, no, I wouldn't call it that. They have had a very hard time.' Later he told Noel Coward that there was nothing so mortifying as to step forward as victor and drop through the stage trap-door.

Not all Tory voters were so sanguine. Eddie Lawrence, a civil servant with the Ministry of Agriculture, wrote of his own prosperous suburb: 'The gloom and despondency that prevailed in Hinchley Wood could not have been greater if we had lost the war. The idea of some of our big industries owned to a large extent by foreigners being owned by the country instead, was nauseating to this patriotic community... Being a civil servant, I have no politics, but I must confess I was somewhat amused at this local depression.'

In the Labour camp the mood was one of exultation. Hugh Dalton, the new Chancellor of the Exchequer, wrote in his diary, 'That first sensation, tingling and triumphant, was of a new society to be built, and we had the power to build it. There was exhilaration among us, joy and hope, determination and confidence. We felt exalted, dedicated, walking on air, walking with destiny.' A columnist in Manchester's Labour journal declared, 'POWER! The *revolution* without a single cracked skull. The pioneers' dreams realized at long last. Nothing to stand in the way of the *socialist* foundation of a new social order.'

Vera Brittain has left us a more homely account of an incident after the election which is equally revealing of well-meaning middle-class condescension and the continuing rigours of austerity Britain: 'Typical was the response of my Chelsea hairdresser, a small middle-aged socialist who had secretly hated the war. He had probably found my visits a relief amongst those of other local residents who did not share his sentiments in that Conservative borough.

'Keeping an appointment shortly after the Labour victory, I found him almost in tears with joy. When I noticed in the window a few packets of scarce "invisible" hairpins and asked if he could spare me one, he seized the precious bundles with both hands and held them out to me. "Take two!" he exclaimed, "Take three! Take four!" and in spite of my protests that I was getting more than my share, the four packets of hairpins were thrust exuberantly into my purse.'

There was to be no 'revolution'. As Arthur Marwick has pointed out, one of the most pleasingly ironic comments on the general election result was provided in November in the pages of Attlee's old school magazine, The Haileyburian and Imperial Service Chronicle. After congratulating a number of old boys on their several political successes it concluded: 'But the School is still more honoured by Mr C. R. Attlee's appointment as Prime Minister, Minister of Defence, and First Lord of the Treasury. This is the first time that any Old Boy has ever filled such high office, and on behalf of the old School, many hundreds of OH's and OISC's, and all those connected with Haileybury and the Imperial Service College, we extend our heartiest congratulations to Mr Attlee, proud that he is a son of Haileybury, and confident that he will not fail his high trust.'

POSTSCRIPT

At the beginning of the first parliamentary session newly elected labour MPs celebrated by singing the Red Flag. A Conservative MP, Oliver Lyttelton, wrote in his memoirs: 'My complacency melted in a minute. I began to fear for my country.' He need not have worried – most of the Labour MPs, then as now, did not know the words.

The artist Sevek's powerful reminder that the war was yet to be won in the Far East.

The election results had confirmed the overwhelming but generally unfocussed desire for change, and a Gallup poll taken shortly afterwards revealed that just 60 per cent of the electorate anticipated that the government would introduce a programme of sweeping reforms. There was little argument – even from the Tories – over the nationalization programme. The coal mines and railways were badly run down after the war, unprofitable sectors of British industry with little appeal to private enterprise. As Attlee recalled, 'of all our nationalization proposals only Iron and Steel aroused much feeling, perhaps because hopes of profit were greater here than elsewhere.'

The nationalization programme itself was rooted firmly in the pre-war tradition of state responsibility and public service corporations. But despite Labour's image as the 'national planning party' it got off to a notably confused start. To his astonishment Manny Shinwell, the new Minister of Fuel, found there was little or nothing to guide him in the nationalization of the mines: 'I enquired whether any documents or blueprints were available at Labour Party headquarters. None was available apart from resolutions advocating public ownership carried at frequent conferences, and a few pamphlets ... presented in general terms.' When nationalization was

above right John Armstrong's 'Can Spring Be Far Behind', painted in 1940, could equally apply to the hopes for a new Europe born out of the ruins of 1945.

above far right A reminder to Germans of the legacies of Nazism, and a warning to Nazis that Nuremberg was only the beginning of the process of law.

right The Japanese surrender aboard the US battleship *Missouri* on 2 September 194

218

The legacy of war. Jewish refugees on their way to a new life in Palestine.

carried through, the old management structures remained virtually intact. The newly formed National Coal Board was chaired by Lord Hyndley, who had previously been the chairman of the largest group of private collieries. No provision was made for workers' representation on any NCB committee above those at pit level. Two years after nationalization the New Statesman commented: 'The Board are remote from the ordinary worker, and the representatives of management with whom he comes into direct contact are nearly all the same persons as before.' At the end of the day 80 per cent of the nation's industry remained in private hands, and in the following decade the nationalized industries became the servants rather than the masters of private industry. Housing, one of the crucial vote-winning issues for Labour during the 1945 election, proved another intractable problem. The government could never meet its target of 400,000 houses a year. By 1948 the number of completed houses lagged behind pre-war levels – 230,000 as compared with a figure of 350,000 for 1938.

There were successes, not least the creation of the National Health Service, which came into being in July 1948. It has always retained an overwhelming popular support, and remains a sacred cow which even the most ideologically committed government is reluctant to lead to the slaughter. There was also a successful export drive, aided to a great extent by the devastation of Japan and Germany. In 1946 industrial production exceeded its highest pre-war level and continued to rise throughout the decade. In spite of continuing austerity at home – most luxury items were 'for export only' – the foundations were laid for the affluence of the 1950s. The bonds of wartime solidarity, so poignantly recalled in Ealing's *Passport to Pimlico* (1949), were slowly being dissolved, and a new kind of society, more prosperous but perhaps more selfish, was about to emerge.

Acknowledgments

The publishers wish to thank those who have given permission for the reproduction of extracts from the following books:

Ancestral Voices
James-Lees Milne, Chatto & Windus

Berlin Twilight
W. Byford Jones, Collins

The Dawn Came Up Like Thunder
Tom Pocock, Collins

Diaries and Letters Harold Nicolson, Penguin

How We Lived Then
Norman Longmate, Hutchinson

I Am My Brother
John Lehmann, Longman

The Rise and Fall of the Third Reich
William Shirer, Secker & Warburg

Westminster at War
William Sansom, Faber

The publishers' thanks are also due to the Mass-Observation Archive for permission to publish extracts.

Picture Acknowledgments

BBC Hulton Picture Library cover, 101, 108, 109, 111 (top), 115 (bottom), 118, 157 (bottom), 168, 209.

BBC Hulton/Bettmann Archive 87, 88.

Robert Capa/Magnum 22, 169.

John Frost Collection title page, 68, 94-5, 122, 206, endpapers.

Robert Hunt Library 8, 16, 17, 19.

Imperial War Museum back cover (top), 6, 15, 24, 25, 27 (top), 30, 39, 44, 47, 54-5, 55, 56, 58, 62, 70, 71 (top), 73 (bottom), 82, 98-9, 103, 107, 115 (top), 117 (bottom), 126, 131, 135 (bottom), 141, 145 (bottom), 146, 150, 152 (top), 155 (top), 158, 159 (bottom), 161 (bottom), 166, 167, 170, 171, 175, 176 (bottom), 178, 179 (bottom), 180, 183, 185, 186, 198, 199, 202 (top right & bottom), 203, 218, 219 (top left).

Leeds Central Library 129, 132.

MacClancy Collection back cover (bottom), 9, 10, 11, 12, 23, 27 (top), 31, 33, 34, 36, 37, 38, 45, 46, 48, 49 (top), 50, 51, 54, 59, 61, 69, 76, 80, 83, 154, 172 (bottom), 182, 191, 202 (top left), 210, 211, 219 (top right & bottom).

Musée des Deux Guerres Mondiales, B.D.I.C. (Université de Paris) 71 (bottom), 138, 139, 142.

National Museum of Photography/Daily Herald Collection 100, 104, 105, 106, 114.

Popperfoto 14, 42, 57, 63, 79, 101, 103, 111, 112, 113, 117, 119, 127, 133 (bottom right), 135, 147, 149, 153 (top), 159, 174, 194, 195, 204-5, 207, 214-5, 216.

Sport & General 79.

Times Newspapers 120-1, 129, 133 (top).

John Topham Library 13, 20, 21, 28, 29, 32, 35, 49 (middle), 52, 53, 60, 64, 65, 72, 73 (top), 77, 86, 89, 106, 125, 145 (top), 148, 152 (bottom), 153, 157 (top), 161 (top), 172 (top), 176 (top), 177, 179 (top), 181, 187, 188, 189, 192, 193, 196, 200-1, 220.

Roger-Viollet 137, 140, 151.

The items on page 123 and 190 are from the Imperial War Museum and the Robert Opie Collection, and were photographed by Angelo Hornak.

Reading List

Addison, Paul *The Road to 1945* (Quartet, 1977)

Attlee, Clement *As It Happened* (Heinemann, 1954)

Barnett, Correlli *The Collapse of British Power* (Eyre Methuen, 1972)

Barr, Charles *Ealing Studios* (David and Charles, 1977)

Bourke-White, Margaret, *Dear Fatherland Rest Quietly* (Simon and Schuster, 1947)

Byford-Jones, W. *Berlin Twilight* (Hutchinson, 1947)

Bullock, Alan *The Life and Times of Ernest Bevin* (Odhams, 1967)

Calder, Angus *The People's War* (Panther, 1971)

Chuikov, V.I. *The End of the Third Reich* (MacGibbon and Kee, 1967)

Cooper, Matthew *The German Army 1939-45* (Macdonald and Jane's, 1978)

Davies, Andrew *Where Did the 40s Go?* (Pluto, 1984)

Erickson, John *The Road to Berlin* (Weidenfeld and Nicolson, 1984)

Fest, Joachim *Hitler* (Pelican, 1977)

Hastings, Max *Bomber Command* (Pan, 1979)

Hattersley, Roy *A Yorkshire Boyhood* (Oxford University Press, 1983)

Henderson, Nicholas *The Private Office* (Weidenfeld and Nicolson, 1984)

Longmate, Norman *When We Won the War* (Hutchinson, 1977)

Liddell Hart, Basil *The Other Side of the Hill* (Pan, 1978)

Marwick, Arthur *The Home Front* (Thames and Hudson, 1976)

Mass-Observation *Peace and the Public* (Longman, 1947)

Mass-Observation *Puzzled People* (Gollancz, 1947)

Mellenthin, Major-General F.W. von, *Panzer Battles* (Futura, 1979)

Nicolson, Harold *Diaries and Letters 1930-64* (Penguin, 1984)

O'Donnell, James P. *The Berlin Bunker* (Arrow, 1979)

Pocock, Tom *The Dawn Came Up Like Thunder* (Collins, 1983)

Ryan, Cornelius *The Last Battle* (New English Library, 1979)

Seabrook, Jeremy *What Went Wrong?* (Gollancz, 1978)

Seaton, Albert *The Fall of Fortress Europe 1943-45* (Batsford, 1981)

Selzer, Michael *Deliverance* (Sphere, 1980)

Speer, Albert *Inside the Third Reich* (Weidenfeld and Nicolson, 1970)

Stevenson, John *British Society 1914-45* (Pelican, 1984)

Trevor Roper, H.R. (ed) *Goebbels' Diaries* (Pan, 1979)

Trevor Roper, H.R. (ed) *Hitler's War Directives* (Pan, 1976)

Trevor Roper, H.R. *The Last Days of Hitler* (Macmillan, 1971)

Warlimont, Walter *Inside Hitler's Headquarters* (Weidenfeld and Nicolson, 1964)

Whiting, Charles *Battle of the Ruhr Pocket* (Ballantine, 1970)

Willmott, H.P. *June 1944* (Blandford, 1984)

Zeimke, Earl F. *Battle for Berlin* (Ballantine, 1968)

Index

Page numbers in italics refer to
  illustrations.